SAGE was founded in 1965 by Sara Miller McCune to support the dissemination of usable knowledge by publishing innovative and high-quality research and teaching content. Today, we publish more than 750 journals, including those of more than 300 learned societies, more than 800 new books per year, and a growing range of library products including archives, data, case studies, reports, conference highlights, and video. SAGE remains majority-owned by our founder, and on her passing will become owned by a charitable trust that secures our continued independence.

Los Angeles | London | Washington DC | New Delhi | Singapore

The Roots of Ill-Governance
and Corruption

Thank you for choosing a SAGE product! If you have any comment, observation or feedback, I would like to personally hear from you. Please write to me at <u>contactceo@sagepub.in</u>

—Vivek Mehra, Managing Director and CEO,
SAGE Publications India Pvt Ltd, New Delhi

Bulk Sales

SAGE India offers special discounts for purchase of books in bulk. We also make available special imprints and excerpts from our books on demand.

For orders and enquiries, write to us at

Marketing Department
SAGE Publications India Pvt Ltd
B1/I-1, Mohan Cooperative Industrial Area
Mathura Road, Post Bag 7
New Delhi 110044, India
E-mail us at <u>marketing@sagepub.in</u>

Get to know more about SAGE, be invited to SAGE events, get on our mailing list. Write today to <u>marketing@sagepub.in</u>

This book is also available as an e-book.

The Roots of Ill-Governance and Corruption

V. Santhakumar

www.sagepublications.com
Los Angeles • London • New Delhi • Singapore • Washington DC

First published in 2015 by

SAGE Publications India Pvt Ltd
B1/I-1 Mohan Cooperative Industrial Area
Mathura Road, New Delhi 110 044, India
www.sagepub.in

SAGE Publications Inc
2455 Teller Road
Thousand Oaks, California 91320, USA

SAGE Publications Ltd
1 Oliver's Yard, 55 City Road
London EC1Y 1SP, United Kingdom

SAGE Publications Asia-Pacific Pte Ltd
3 Church Street
#10-04 Samsung Hub
Singapore 049483

Published by Vivek Mehra for SAGE Publications India Pvt Ltd, typeset in 10/13 Palatino by RECTO Graphics, Delhi and printed at Sai Print-o-Pack, New Delhi.

Library of Congress Cataloging-in-Publication Data Available

ISBN: 978-93-515-0059-9 (HB)

The SAGE Team: N. Unni Nair, Sanghamitra Patowary, Anju Saxena and Rajinder Kaur

Contents

List of Tables and Boxes

Tables

Boxes

Preface

How do we achieve 'good governance' in India? Many well-meaning people seem to think that this can be achieved through better laws or legal mechanisms (such as the Lokpal) or by installing a 'strong' leader at the helm of affairs. What is 'good governance' then? For private investors, quicker decisions by the government to facilitate their investments, including the provision of land by the state without allowing much social opposition, is good governance. Media talks about the positive impact of good governance when chief ministers are re-elected twice or thrice in situations, such as in Delhi or Bihar, without thinking about what 'good governance' means in these different contexts. We, the sections of the middle class, see the programmes to provide money or support for food or employment to sections of the society as populist (and somewhat unnecessary), and think that 'strong leaders' can avoid such expenditure programmes without understanding the compulsions of democracy or democratisation. We take a moral view of politicians as good or bad, or strong or weak (probably like the characters in Mahabharata or Ramayana), and do not see the social conditions that shape them and their policies. In general, the public understanding of the role of democracy and the process of democratisation is not well informed in India, and that shapes our views on what is good governance and how to accomplish it.

Ideally, these notions have to be corrected by basic social sciences which may be taught to all, starting from schools. Otherwise, these should be part of public debates at all levels. However, I do not see social scientists carrying out this task well in India. There could be a number of historical reasons. It is true that a major section of Indian social scientists (including sociologists, political scientists, political economists, historians and so on) had a clear understanding of the need for studying historical evolution of societies including their forms of governance. They were very active in public discussions and efforts to create social awareness on such issues. However, they were influenced by Marxism and its propositions on how societies might evolve and, what should be done to accelerate that evolution. Given this background and the historical failure of socialist experiment, Indian social scientists (and their counterparts in many parts of the developing world) were at a loss to understand the nature of democratic evolution that might have taken place in non-socialist societies. Many continued with the (fading) hopes on socialism, cursing the neoliberal assertion. However, they could not communicate a reliable story to the Indian population on the possible transition of politics in India and similar countries. Moreover, people at large have lost interest in, or are not convinced of the need of, a socialist future. Good scholarship in political science and sociology based on liberal and/or non-socialist or non-Marxist framework is scarce in India.

Economists, especially those who are not wedded to Marxist thought, are the potential candidates to provide a different story of social transition to the people. However, non-Marxist economists in general have confined themselves to analyse specific social contexts (with the help of theory and/or empirical evidence) and have highlighted 'ideal' policies based partly on their ideological moorings on the differing role of the state. Understanding the dynamics of the situation and predicting a path of evolution of the economy and society have not been attempted often by non-Marxist economists in India.

It is in this context, I am trying to sketch a long-run story of the evolution of good governance in this book, aimed at a wider audience, and not exclusively for social scientists or academics.

Different phases of my academic experience contribute to the writing of this book. I was fascinated by the dynamics of institutional evolution (and the bottlenecks in the path of such evolution) from the beginning of my academic life as a doctoral student. I also had opportunities to study, in a systematic manner, how different societies respond differently to proposals of institutional reforms (Santhakumar, 2008). There were also close interactions with the local governments of Kerala to facilitate what can be called 'good governance'.[1] As a consultant to multilateral organisations,[2] I could see governments in different countries responding differently to the needs of their citizens, and also to proposals for improving the situation.

Beyond all these assignments, the writing of this book draws on my experience as a keen observer and commentator[3] of the politics and governance in Kerala—a state which has achieved higher levels of human development much ahead of other states in India, and is, also, currently one of the fastest growing regional economies within the country. There are many other firsts of Kerala—which are not well recognised in the debates on human development—a state which could elect a non-Congress government in India in the fifties, a state which moved to real competitive democracy for the first time in India, a state which was forced to adopt many policies a number of decades ago which we consider populist today, where such 'populism' was noted for its negative impact on investments and economic growth, where the real competition in politics is such that the two competing political coalitions followed by and large similar set of policies, where the population currently comprises of a substantial section of the middle class, where the interest of this class and the media catering to them create problems for politicians who get into corruption scandals and so on. Many problems that we discuss at the national level today (populism, governance failure, public attention on corruption, negative impact on investment climate, etc.) were the subjects of public debates in Kerala from the seventies onwards. After going through a phase of such populist-driven governance 'failure' for decades, the state is currently witnessing a growth phase drawing on the achievements in human development, probably driven by the policies of populism. Hence, the story of Kerala may have lessons for India

---

[1] As part of the Research Unit on Local Self-Government at the Centre for Development Studies, Trivandrum (Kerala), we carried out a two-year project in one district of Kerala to help village and district panchayats to improve their service delivery and governance.

[2] Mainly to the Asian Development Bank and United Nations Environment Programme.

[3] I write a regular column in the online version of a major newspaper in local language.

as a whole and many other parts of the world,[4] not necessarily the way it has been told earlier, including the excellent accounts given by Amartya Sen and his collaborators.

I got support from a number of people in this venture. The academic space provided by the Azim Premji University (APU) for such writing projects is exemplary. Giridhar and Manoj, of the university, arranged an editor, named Ashok Chandran, for the first typescript who had provided valuable feedback, although I could not restructure the book completely according to his suggestions. My long association with the Centre for Development Studies (CDS), Trivandrum (which continues even today as a visiting faculty) is the major source of learning and reflection on Kerala. Research on service delivery that is included in this book was carried out with the funding of the Research Unit on Local Self-Government of CDS, and K. Narayanan Nair was gracious in extending all the support. I remember an ex-colleague in CDS, Ravi Raman, who brought my attention to the positive role of the middle class in response to my presentation on how this class is cornering a major part of the public subsidies provided for electricity and water. Research that became part of this book was presented in different forums: Centre for Development Studies, Trivandrum; APU, Bangalore; Jadavpur University, Kolkata; India Development Foundation and Jawaharlal Nehru University, Delhi. The comments received in these seminars, especially those from Dwaipayan Bhattacharyya, Indraneel Dasgupta, A. Narayana, Shubhashis Gangopadhyay, Achin Chakraborty and others, helped to sharpen the arguments, and I am not implicating any of them for what is written in the book. Parts of the typescript were used for teaching a course on 'political economy, development and governance' in APU, and clarifying the doubts of students helped a lot in reordering and revising the arguments. The insightful suggestions received from the anonymous referee arranged by SAGE helped a lot in revising the book. This book is dedicated to Praveena Kodoth—a friend who has shaped my understanding of gender issues.

---

[4] Jeffrey (2008) has noted some of these parallels between Kerala in the past and the country today.

1

Introduction

The 'immodest' claim in this book is that it analyses some fundamental hurdles that the attempts to improve governance or reduce corruption may encounter in developing countries, such as India. The public debates that are going on in India at the time of writing this book also stress the need for understanding these fundamental constraints, and not the symptoms. The year 2012 started with a middle-class led agitation against corruption in the country. The proponents of such agitation wanted a new law or legal mechanism (namely, Lokpal) against corruption. It should be clearer to those who think a little more systematically that the absence of one or the other law or legal mechanism could not be the reason for the prevalence of corruption in India. This is so because there are a number of laws or legal mechanisms to tackle corruption that already exist, but are unused or underused by the society. We have seen that people are electing corruption-linked politicians, despite these highly visible campaigns.

The year also witnessed a slowdown of economic growth, declining value of rupee and warnings about India's economic situation by credit-rating agencies. Then the attention of the public debates was focussed on the role of some 'populist' politicians, so-called 'inability' of the prime minister and the lack of political will on the part of the ruling party to go ahead with economic reforms. There was very little attention on the socio-economic factors that made political decision making slow and tedious, created populist politicians and made political parties unwilling to go ahead with growth-oriented reforms. If governance is in a crisis, there could be some underlying socio-economic reasons, and we need to think about them.

This book attempts to use the theoretical insights of economics to understand the real world political barriers against improving governance. The relationship between politics or the process of democratisation and governance is analysed here in a more nuanced manner. For example, there are situations where a deepening of democracy leads to a decline in the quality of 'governance', as understood in a particular manner. For example, when two parties compete intensely in a developing society, each may offer a wider set of private goods (see Box 1.1) at subsidised rates to different sections of society or voters, and they need not necessarily be poor. This is called competitive populism, and it may have a negative impact on certain aspects of governance, say, the provision of public goods (Box 1.1) which are expected from a well-functioning government.

As part of competitive populism, there could also be a negative impact on the fiscal situation of the government. This possibility—

Box 1.1:
Private versus Public Goods

Private goods are, in general, excludable and divisible. For example, an apple when consumed by one person is not available to others. Moreover, it is easy for a supplier not to give an apple to someone who is not paying for it. On the other hand, the service of a street light (part of public goods) can be consumed by a number of people, or one person's consumption does not affect the consumption of (a few) others. It is difficult to exclude somebody from using a street light. It is generally expected in economics that markets, and not governments, should supply private goods. Proper public goods are those which are indivisible and non-excludable, such as defence service or light houses. Nobody can be excluded from enjoying the benefits of these services, and one person's consumption does not reduce the availability of the service for others. However, there are many goods and services which have varying degrees of indivisibility and non-excludability. All these are considered as public goods in this context. Moreover, there can be services, such as schooling or healthcare, which are not public goods in conventional sense, but these are also provided by the government (as public services) in many societies. Here, we consider all those goods and services conventionally provided by the government.

Source: Author.

competitive populism negatively affecting governance—needs to be understood without underestimating the importance of the process of democratisation (or the deepening of democracy) that leads to competitive populism. Moreover, a competitive distribution of private goods may be needed to enhance the consumption basket of the poorer sections of the society, and this may be leading to higher levels of social or human development despite its negative impact on certain aspects of governance, such as the provision of public goods. How do societies get out of competitive populism without undermining democracy? This book attempts to address this question.

However, this book is not written as a research monograph. It is attempting to tell a 'grand' story of political transition that may happen in different contexts, and how it may affect governance and corruption. Although situations within the same country at different points of time and those within different countries are compared anecdotally, there is no systematic data-based hypothesis testing attempted here. Given the vast differences between countries on a number of parameters, it may be difficult to test these hypotheses systematically. The purpose of the book is to propose some insightful hypotheses (which can be contested through public debates and/or systematic research) on the possible links between political transition and the nature of governance. The targeted audience of the book is general readers—including politicians, journalists, civil society activists and public at large who do not have a formal training in economics or political science, but are intrigued by the problems of ill-governance and corruption encountered by countries, such as India.

Defining Governance

Although there have been attempts to understand government within economics, governance is yet to get a widely accepted definition within economics. There is a view of governance as 'the structuring and functioning of the legal and social institutions that support economic activity and economic transactions by protecting property rights, enforcing contracts and taking collective action to provide physical and organisational infrastructure' (Dixit, 2009). Accordingly, governance and governments are to be viewed differently since there can be means other than the government to perform the role of governance, especially when the governments do not exist or fail to carry out the expected tasks adequately. Informal norms, communitarian institutions and sometimes coercive non-state actors (such as mafia) may be substituting or complementing the governments in the provision of 'governance'.

Since property rights enforcement of contracts and mechanisms facilitating collective action are enabling institutions (or formal or informal rules of the game), governance can be viewed as creating, managing and changing these institutions (wherever such change is needed). This would be the working definition of governance used in this book.

However, for a reader not used to the jargons of economics, we need to elaborate what is meant by good governance in this book. Some of the features of good governance are:

1. The major focus of a 'good government' has to be the provision of public goods, such as infrastructure. This is so because individuals cannot provide such public goods efficiently and adequately and if governments too do not provide them, the society will be deprived of adequate supply of such goods. This may dampen the prospects for sustained improvements in social welfare and economic development.

2. Create and enforce rules in those cases where markets or voluntary actions of individuals are inadequate to enhance social welfare. This includes the maintenance of law and order in society and the protection of rights of individuals. Monopoly is also such a case where market by itself is inadequate, and, hence, controlling monopoly when it creates net social losses can be part of the expected role of the government.

3. There is a need for the provision of private goods or money or distribution of assets to the poor or those who cannot

make a decent life on their own. However, such transfers should not aim at specific individuals as a way of harnessing electoral support; rather it should aim at those groups of people who have certain features so that they cannot participate adequately on their own in income-generation activities. Such transfer programmes would also see a reduction or change in their coverage, as and when the targeted groups come out of their difficult or special situations.

4. There has to be accountability measures to ensure that private interests do not lead to not-so-desirable impact on public interests. This is to be achieved through separation of powers of different stakeholders, so that the socially harmful impacts of conflict of interest and concentration of power are minimised.

5. Although it is implied here, it is to be mentioned that the government has a role to ensure the rights of all citizens and that public services due to individuals are delivered in a transparent manner.

These ideas of good governance, mentioned here, are those of liberal democracy or political and economic liberalism. There are other academic and popular notions of good governance. For example, good governance is seen by some people in terms of the speed in which investment proposals of the capitalists are cleared, even if this is done by dictatorial rulers or in contexts where the rights of certain groups of the society are violated. The idea of governance driving the socialist states before their collapse in the early nineties was that government had to regulate all consumption- and production-related decisions of citizens. Even today, one can hear politicians in India talking about the responsibility of the state in providing petroleum fuels at subsidised rates to citizens. This book does not subscribe to views of such expanded roles of the government as an 'ideal' form of governance. However, it explores the internal conditions of society which create adequate stakeholders who demand liberal-democratic governance or which facilitate a movement away from other notions of governance described here.

The Basic Argument

Like a few other political scientists writing on the subject of governance, I have also categorised certain key phases or stages in politics and governance of the developing economies. The starting point is 'elite capture' in which not only the governance, but also a greater part of the resources (including those like minerals) are kept under the custody of the elites. Here, the elite can be social and/or economic. They provide public goods, such as roads and infrastructure for themselves, take rent from public resources, such as land and minerals, and carry out some minimal transfer of private goods or money to the ruled majority. The rules by the kings and colonialists are by and large examples of elite capture. However, elite capture can prevail even if there is formal democracy, especially if there is no effective competition to the ruling party or the ruler.[1] If the survival of the ruling elites does not depend on the support from below (as in a non-democratic situation), a greater part of public resources can be used for the consumption of the elites (including public goods aimed at them). Sections of the ruled may get access to these public goods due to the inherently non-excludable nature of these goods, but their demand for public goods is also likely to be low due to their lower consumption of private goods. There is an assumption here of a positive relationship between the demand for public goods and private consumption. If someone is too poor and, hence, worried about the next meal, he/she may not be concerned much about the poor quality of the village road.

Elite capture may characterise a close collaboration between the capitalists and the ruling elites. The capitalists can be from within or outside the country. Ruling domestic elites may share resources with the foreign capitalists. In certain cases, domestic rulers may be subservient to foreign capitalists or their army, and this becomes colonialism. The ruling elites and the limited capitalist class within

---

[1] There can be vote-bank politics where individuals from sections of society follow a leader or a party.

the country can also be one and the same. Hence, there can be different forms of elite capture, but its basic economic character in terms of governance can be similar. It is aimed at the needs of the ruling elite, and there can be some transfer of private goods to the ruled depending on the need for support from below and the benevolence of the rulers.

In the next stage, the elites who control the state are overthrown or changed violently or peacefully—through democratic or non-democratic means—by one or other form of, what can be called, counter-elites. There can be different forms of this counter-elite capture. Independence or freedom struggles could be one. This could also be an assertion of the domestic elite over foreigners, but such societies may gradually witness counter-elite assertions against the ruling domestic elites. There could be under-class asser-tion wherein people belonging to economically under-privileged groups assert over the ruling economic elite. This is what has hap-pened under the leadership of the socialist or communist parties. There could also be an assertion by oppressed social groups, such as lower castes against the upper castes which control the state.

This change or transition—or counter-elite capture—can lead to greater control of public resources by the non-elite sections of the society. They may try to corner a greater share of the rent from public assets either for the class or group they represent or for the leaders themselves. Since the leaders need support from below to come to power in the first place and to continue there under normal circumstances, counter-elite capture may lead to a wider sharing of public resources. There could be a change in the allocation of private goods. The ruled majority may get more private goods, as the state controlled by the counter-elites may be giving more to all or to some groups which were not getting much previously under elite capture. Such provision of private goods is a part of fulfilling the aspirations of people who have supported the removal of elites from the control of the state. Hence, counter-elite capture can widen the coverage of resource transfer from the state to society. This has implications for the economy. Since the very limited consumption of private goods (including education) of major sections of soci-ety has a dampening effect on economic development in general, the expansion of private goods consumption facilitated through counter-elite capture may have favourable implications for the economy. Hence, counter-elite capture has to be seen as serving an instrumental or functional role too, in addition to the inherent virtues of such a process of democratisation (or wider participation of society in the process of democracy).

The relationship between the counter-elites and capitalist class is a dynamic one. Although the former may take an adversarial position against those capitalists who were very close to (or part of) the previously ruling elite, capitalist enterprises are needed to generate wealth unless the counter-elites go for a full-fledged state control of productive enterprises as in the socialist countries. Whether it is through state-owned enterprises or through encouraging another capitalist class or by building new relationship with the prevailing domestic or foreign capitalists, counter-elites would build up an institutional base for production. It is possible that the leaders of counter-elites may gradually become elite economically (due to the rent from public resources) and may become even social elites (especially when social hierarchy is in tune with economic or power hierarchy), but then they may face another counter-elite capture.

When the previously ruling elites have not been eradicated completely and the counter-elites have established themselves politically, there can be a competition between these two political formations. Alternatively, if the previous elites have been eradicated then the counter-elite capture may turn out to be 'elite capture' and it may, over a period of time, encounter another aggressive counter-elite. In a system wherein elites and counter-elites compete, such competition requires widening of one's support base. Even if this competition is not manifested through democratic elections but through periodical (violent or non-violent) 'regime-changing' revolutions, such widening of support base is needed. However, in societies which have formally accepted democracy, electoral competition takes root through this process.

In the early phase of this competitive democracy in a developing economy, the focus is somewhat inevitably on the distribution of private goods. This can be called competitive populism. Each of the competing groups is likely to amass resources from the society or publicly owned assets, and distribute among its actual and potential support base. Usually in developing societies, the direct tax system is less likely to be developed. This may lead to greater dependence on indirect taxes and other resources which form public assets. There can also be a changing nature of what is considered to be public assets. For example, a position of government job can also be reckoned as a public asset. In certain cases, private assets (say, land) may be captured to convert them into state-owned or public assets.

The distribution of (or transfer of money for) private goods could account for the major expenditure with public resources then. The competition in this regard between two political formations would lead to an increase in the quantum and coverage of such distribution. When a party representing the poor and the other party representing the affluent sections compete, both may try to shape their agenda to get the support of those voters who are somewhere in the middle (neither poor nor affluent) to get the majority. Hence, the competition can mean a dominance of the median voter in certain cases. The private goods demands of the median voter may get undue attention by the competing elites and counter-elites (or competing political formations) in a developing society.[2]

What are the impacts of such competition between the elite and counter-elite on economy? This competition may enhance the private goods consumption of the ruled majority, and this can be beneficial for the economy as long as their low private consumption is a constraint on economic development. Thus, the constraints imposed on economic growth or social/human development due to undernourishment, illiteracy and ill health of a large section of the society may be overcome at this stage. Hence, competitive populism may be playing an important role in achieving minimal development indicators like those considered in the calculation of Human Development Index (HDI). This book puts forward an argument that the achievement of higher level of HDI in Kerala ahead of other Indian states or in other Indian states,

---

[2] On the other hand, median voter's preference over the combination of public goods and taxes may influence the electoral agenda in developed democracies.

such as Tamil Nadu, later on, can be linked to the emergence of competitive populism in these contexts. The competition between elites and counter-elites may result in some competition between the capitalists too. Hence, the social loss associated with the crony or monopoly capitalism is likely to decline in such politically competitive societies. However, this competitive populism can lead to an under-provision of public goods and an increase in the debt burden of their governments.

Expanding private goods consumption among the ruled would gradually increase their demand for public goods. This is not merely due to the direct impact of increased consumption of private goods provided by the state. If education is also provided widely as part of the 'distribution' policy, it will enhance the demand for jobs and private investments for creating such jobs. The lack of adequate public goods can become a major constraint against private investments and economic growth, and the income-earning opportunities of the population at large. On the other hand, if the incomes of people increase, this also leads to an increased demand for public goods. Hence, a wider distribution of private goods can enhance the demand for public goods over a period of time.

However, in a phase of competitive populism, the state's ability to expand the provision of public goods is limited as it cannot avoid expanding or reducing the coverage of resource transfer for private goods, as it is competing with the other to be in power. It may take time for the society to convey signals to the parties competing for power to focus more on providing public goods and less on transfer for private goods. This evolution is a slow process and can be debilitated by getting trapped into a competitive but inefficient equilibrium.

The transition from elite capture to counter-elite capture and then towards competitive democracy (or populism) have important implications for governance. It could be that governance in certain aspects (including the provision of public goods, other public services and rule of law) was somewhat 'better' (compared to the demands of the society) under elite capture in certain situations. There is a rationale for this expectation. If the elites belong to higher-income groups, they may demand higher level of public goods, and these could be provided according to their wishes in a state of elite capture even by neglecting the private goods needs of the ruled majority. Such provision of public goods could be an indicator of 'good governance'. On the other hand, the elites may not have adequate incentives to regulate monopoly capitalism—and such regulation can also be reckoned as an indicator of good governance—since the beneficiaries of such monopoly could be part of these ruling elites.

On the other hand, there can be a decline or degeneration in certain dimensions of governance (say, the provision of public service or infrastructure) as part of the counter-elite capture due to the need to use more resources for private goods transfer. This may continue or worsen as a part of the competitive populism. Hence, such a transition towards counter-elite capture and then to populist competition due to a process of politicisation and demo-cratisation, though, is useful in its own, but expecting it to result in 'good governance' immediately is unrealistic. Therefore, it could be incorrect to expect democratisation and good governance to move in the same direction always.

Some instruments for achieving good governance, such as 'citizens' charters', may not be used by the citizens neither under elite capture nor under counter-elite capture or competitive popu-lism, even if such instruments are in place. This is so because the relationship between citizens and politicians (or the government) can be of a different kind in different contexts. Under elite capture, citizens (or the ruled majority) may expect 'something' from the state based on the benevolence of the ruler. Under counter-elite capture, those citizens who have supported such capture expect rewards, including private goods (and a share of public resources for private benefit), and not merely good governance. Under com-petitive populism, voters expect the parties to distribute private goods or carry out cash transfer as promised during the elections.

Moreover, those who expect private goods from the counter-elite or populist governments usually develop a personal relationship with politicians at different levels. Populist politicians are not interested in creating a transparent rule and allow the officials to deliver private goods without any intervention. There has to be enough scope for discretion at different levels to signal that it is not the 'neutral' government that delivers these goods, but it is due to the intervention of the particular politician for the benefit of the specific citizen or group. It is through this process that the mutual 'give and take' relationship between the politician and the voter gets established. This relationship that prevails for private goods may be used for getting public services too. When a citizen wants a license to construct a house from the local government, he/she may want to use the prevailing 'give and take' relationship that prevails with the politician, rather than expecting the government to deliver the service dispassionately and simply based on the rule. In sum, the ways used by citizens to get service from politicians can be different in different political contexts and in certain contexts, citizens' charters or similar instruments need not be used even if they exist. In such contexts, even if these instruments exist, an improvement in governance or service delivery based on them need not take place. The use of instruments to improve governance, without understanding the political context, may lead to surprisingly unpleasant results. This is true for other accountability measures, including public forums or even citizen assemblies to scrutinise public expenditure or the right to information act or formal anti-corruption measures.

The pattern of corruption is also similar to that of governance in general. Under elite capture, the notion of corruption itself could be different. The ruling elites using public resources for their own benefits need not be seen as 'corruption' then. When the counter-elites come to power, they may imitate the previously ruled elites in the use of public resources for their own needs. The counter-elites may distribute this right to use public resources or to extract rent from public assets or positions to a wider group of their 'henchmen' at different levels. Competitive populism may deepen this process to some extent, but those who sit in opposition may raise the issue of the excessive use of public resources by the ruling party without much in-principle opposition to such use. The political competition and each trying to raise allegations of corruption against other, correctly or bogusly, may gradually bring corruption into the public domain. However, whether such stories of corruption lead to the voting out of the ruling party (and, hence, become a deterrent for political parties) depends on other factors.

This book highlights that there is a disconnection between economic growth and good governance. The lack of 'good governance' need not be a constraint for higher levels of economic growth. There can be capitalist growth under elite capture, counter-elite capture and populist competition. This happens if the capitalist class is not affected much due to poor governance. They may either develop close personal relationships with politicians to get over the problems of poor governance or develop alternative means of overcoming the scarcity of public goods or other constraints. Thus, the lack of good governance should not be seen in terms of its impact on economic growth per se.

However, there can be issues related to the quality of growth. There can be lack of inclusiveness or some sections of society may not benefit much from economic growth. It is this inclusiveness that happens, albeit slowly, through political transition from elite capture to counter-elite capture and then to competitive populism. It is not that all such issues of non-inclusiveness would be addressed in competitive populism. There can be failures in such societies in extending social security and basic private goods or merit goods to the poor, especially when competitive populism demands the distribution of non-basic private goods to a wider section of society, and not only to the poor.

How do governments move away from a focus on transfer for private goods to the provision of public goods? The phase where democracy matures and the competition between the political parties is mainly about the provision of public goods (or tax and public goods combinations), and not much about the distribution of private goods, is called 'liberal democracy' here. Moving towards such a regime requires changes in social demand. It would mean that at the individual level, people should be willing to trade off the currently received private goods from the state for more public goods. At the aggregate level, there should be a significant section in society seeing such trade-off beneficial. Moreover, the electoral competition would mean that the important classes in electoral politics (sometimes this can be the median voter) should see such a change as beneficial. Such a change in the demand of people should be sensed by the competing political parties.

It is argued here that such a change in demand occurs through the emergence of a middle class which depends on markets for their consumption, wages and investment. Then they will develop incentives to demand good governance as understood within the framework used in this book. Hence, the political willingness to bring in good governance depends on the electoral importance of this middle class. Examples are taken from Indian states and other countries where such middle class plays a crucial role in electoral politics, and hence enable some visible changes in terms of improving governance and reducing corruption.

However, somewhat ironically, such a middle class emerges out of the policies of distributing private goods, including education facilitated through counter-elite capture and competitive populism. Hence, it is through the populism that societies come out of populism! Despite the emergence of such a middle class in India as a whole during the last two decades, their percentage and role in many states of India are limited. The continuation of high levels of ill- governance and corruption in India is explained here in terms of this less important role that this class has on the electoral politics that shapes the central government, and also many state governments in India.

In one sense, this book re-politicises the debate on governance from a liberal economic perspective. This is important since the critique of economists' efforts to improve governance in the developing world was that they had attempted a depoliticised approach focussing on decentralisation, non-state actors (such as civil society) and the use of instruments, such as citizens' charters. In that sense, this book shares the criticism that such non-politicisation is not helping even if the objective is to have good governance, as understood within mainstream economics. Thus, the book holds on to the need for 'good governance' as in liberal economic paradigm, but articulates the constraints in this regard in terms of the slow pace of political transition or the lack of a social and political demand for such good governance.

The remaining part of the book is organised as follows. The chapters, which follow, deal with each stage of the political transition, especially its impact on the allocation of public resources, governance and corruption. Elite capture is discussed in Chapter 2. Two types of counter-elite capture are discussed in Chapters 3 and 4: The first type is social counter-elites, such as a middle or lower caste group in a context where the elites consist of upper castes and the second type is under-class political formations, such as the working class (or socialist/communist) parties. This is followed by a discussion on competitive populism in Chapter 5. A discussion on how societies come out of competitive populism is in Chapter 6. Major lessons are summarised in the last chapter.

2

Elite Capture

There are many books written on states or governments which reflect different degrees of what can be called elite capture.[1] There is no attempt here to repeat or rewrite whatever has been written in this regard. The purpose of this chapter is a very limited one: It tries to understand governance in those elite-captured states in the overall framework used in this book.

Who Are the Elites, and How Do They Capture the State?

In most societies, government or its crude form could be first established by a small section of people who belongs to elites or those representing them. By elite, we mean a relatively small section of people who have unusual power or authority. They acquire or retain the power due to superiority in physical violence, wealth, religious or ritual status and so on. One can always ask the question whether these people have become the elites after acquiring power or that they have acquired power due to their elite

[1] Elite capture of the state is well discussed in the literature. The influence of the dominant class on the state is discussed in Marxist political economy (for example, see Alavi, 1972; Poulantzas, 1969; Bardhan, 1984). The discussion was on whether the state is fully dependent on the dominant class or has some autonomy. Lieten (1996) sees cases of elite capture in the local governments in India. Bardhan et al. (2009) also discuss elite capture as a benchmark for understanding the political transition of societies.

position. Even in a context where there is no one who is elite, to start with, it is difficult to imagine some among them acquiring ruling authority without the help of certain legitimacy or power. Superiority in physical violence might help a set of people to acquire power, and here we can take them as elite in terms of violence. Such superiority in violence comes with better mobilisation of armed men or tools.

However, superiority in physical violence and the upper hand in other matters go hand-in-hand. Some may start using superiority in physical violence to take over assets used or held by others (probably land, cattle, water bodies, etc.). This capturing of assets may turn 'elites in terms of violence' into 'elites in terms of wealth' (even before the capture of the state). There could also be elites in terms of rituals or religion. They may develop either a non-adversarial relationship with elites in terms of violence or wealth, or the former may be controlled or superseded by the latter. These two sections of elites could also be one and the same. It is not common to see a situation in the past where elites in terms of rituals or religion (or theology) established its supremacy and captured the state against the interest of elites in terms of violence and/or wealth.

Although there could be several manifestations of elite capture in a society, elites who control the state are more likely to have established some control over physical violence of others (with either formal military or informal armed groups) and the wealth of the region or society, and they are likely to have support from sections of religious or ritual elites. Or there is some cooperation between different sections of elites, and the situation is not the one in which each section of elite is in continuous fight with the other. This is an improvement over the pre-existing situation—before the formation of the state—where each group led by sections of elite is in constant tussle with the other, there are many groups using violence against the other and there is no state which can (coercively) control the violence of different groups.

One explanation for the emergence of such a state and the (fragile) cooperation of different sections of elites is given in North et al. (1998). They cite this as the emergence of *Limited Access Order*.

In this situation, access to political and economic competition, and organisations supported by the state is restricted. This restricted competition gives rent to those who have access to them. They need to preserve these rents. Thus, they need to collectively preserve the order and the different sections of elites who have access to different activities (such as religious rituals, warfare, trade, etc.) have an interest in collaborating, rather than being in constant confrontation. The way the caste system limited access to religious rituals, trade, warfare, etc. to specific groups in India could be one such example. However, there may arise situations where the conflicts between these collaborating elites may sharpen, and such conflict may lead either to: (a) a regression in terms of statehood—a move towards the anarchic situation that prevailed before the establishment of the elite captured state; or (b) to a new equilibrium of collaborative relationship between different sections of the elite.

Response of the Ruled Majority in Elite Capture

There would be periods where the 'high-handedness' of the ruling elites would be tolerated by the majority or the ruled. Their expectation from the state or the government could be minimal at its very early stages. (The idea that the state or the government has to provide many things to its citizens is a very recent concept in the history of governance.) These expectations could be limited to certain basic public goods, such as the protection from violent robbers. Citizenry could also be an evolving concept, and there can be stages where every individual in society need not be seen as a citizen who can 'demand' public services from the state. Even in modern economies, household is reckoned as a single unit in terms of the provision of services. In the early stages of governance, the state had relationships with much larger units—these could be regional satraps or feudal landlords around whom used to be a large number of households or clusters of people, such as tenants, workers and those sharing kinship ties. A part of the protection from the violent robbers was provided by these smaller units themselves. But they would have demanded additional protection against the state, say, from major invading armies, as there could be some economy of scale in providing such protection, and any single unit organising such additional protection has to bear huge costs.

One can broadly divide the ruled majority into two: (a) landlords and people working for them; and (b) urban producers or traders and people working with them. These are in addition to the ruling elite (and those linked directly with them), and it is possible that the ruling elite may share a close relationship with (a) and/or (b).

Provision of Private Goods

A major part of the private goods transfer—by which we mean the support for subsistence or for avoiding or reducing poverty of the people—was organised within (a) and (b). This was then rarely carried out by the state. Thus, the physically disabled worker or the aged worker may be expecting support from his family or kinship or from the landlord, and not much from the state. Hence, the overall demand for private goods transfer from the state was minimal then.

However, the people who are directly depending on the ruling elite (officials, soldiers and so on), taking care of their private goods requirements could be an important part of the governance under elite capture. Support for religious and similar organisations also come under this category. Dissatisfaction among the people, aiding the ruler, could be a potential threat to the ruling elite. In general, the elite-captured states encounter the need to transfer public resources for the private goods consumption of themselves and the people directly depending on or aiding them. They rarely encounter the need to meet the private goods requirement of the people at large (as in the case of democratic governments of developing countries).

Provision of Public Goods and Governance under Elite Capture

The rural landlords and urban traders or industrialists could be expecting some protection from the ruling elite. They would collaborate with the ruling elite if this is provided. There could be foreigners also among these urban traders who seek protection from the ruling elite. If landlords and traders saw a reduction in protection from the ruling elite despite giving them resources, this could lead to a potential threat against the sustenance of the latter.

In return for the protection, the ruling elite got resources from the landlords and traders as taxes and non-tax incomes, in addition to the rent that the elite received through their control of state-owned or state-acquired assets. If the tax collection system was less developed, a greater part of the income for the ruler would have come from state-owned assets, or there could be an acquisition of properties by the ruler with this purpose.

Among the public goods that rural land owners expect from the government, irrigation is important. This is important in regions where expansion or intensification of cultivation requires irrigation. There are theories which see the need for irrigation as the one driving the need for establishing a state or kingdom (Service, 1978). There is a coordination problem in the provision of irrigation, and here the complexity increases as the scale of (optimal) irrigation expands. For areas where small-scale irrigation is possible and adequate, coordination problems could be solved at the level of village or kinships. However, there are geographical areas where large-scale irrigation systems are needed and are cheaper, and a large-scale coordinating mechanism is important. Early forms of government (which were controlled by the elites) played an important role in this regard. Rural traders or those who reared livestock might have demanded protection against those who were likely to take away their property.

If we take the protection of private property as an important part of public goods, the major function of the state ruled by the elite is the provision of such protection. Hence, the state was important for the propertied classes: those who have immobile properties (such as landlords) and those having mobile ones (such as traders). There could be a demand for infrastructural public goods in the cities by the urban traders or industrialists and the ruling elite themselves. The demand for public goods by the workers or the dependents (that is, substantial section of population) could be minimal for two reasons: (a) Their private goods consumption itself could be small, and that may reflect in their minimal demand for public goods—assuming a positive relationship between consumption of private goods and public goods; (b) A part of their public goods consumption would be subsumed under the public goods consumption of the urban traders, industrialists and the elites. This is so because the public goods available for traders or elites will be available to the people at large too due to the indivisibility and non-excludability features of such goods. This is especially so when there are no mechanisms to exclude them from using public goods. (It may be noted that caste-based exclusion existed in India on the use of roads, ponds and other such public goods.)

Economic Growth and Elite Capture

The elites ruling the state could implement growth-oriented economic policies (facilitating greater private investments) if they desired to do so. This depended on the incentives of the ruling elite and the gains that they could derive from such growth. The possibility of monopoly and the political possibilities in sharing the profit by the ruling elites would encourage them to expand production and/or exchange. Hence, this expansion of commerce under elite capture need not translate into the development of a competitive economy, since the elites would prefer monopoly. Even if this might create certain social losses (and a reduction in consumer welfare), this would not hamper economic growth much.

One can relate the potential for economic growth under elite capture to the ideas in economic growth theory. Growth requires higher savings and investments. Elites were in a position to tap greater savings from the economy for investments. This might have come from the state's ownership or not-so-contested control over other resources. Alternatively, the rulers were able to provide a conducive environment to capitalists (even from outside) by sharing the potential gains of their investments. However, if the production or commerce depended on domestic consumption, the wealth status of the majority of people could become a binding constraint. Hence, the growth-oriented elites would have an interest in tapping foreign markets. This could be for selling the commodities as well as for attracting or mobilising investments or inputs. Elites would develop close relationship with a few foreign investors, but it need not be a free-for-all situation for the latter. Thus, the elite-captured economy need not be a closed one. Openness of these economies was likely to manifest in the export of primary commodities initially, since local value addition might have required skilled workers and other intermediate inputs, and these might need investments, institution building, etc. This is so because it would take time for social investments and social change to build an adequate supply of skilled workers and intermediate inputs for domestic value addition.

In summary, we should understand that elites capturing the state have certain 'advantages' in terms of provision of public goods. These include: (a) They do not have to spend much money on private goods of the people at large, and this part of the money could be used for public goods; (b) They do not have to really take into account the public goods needs of the wider section of the population. Thus, they may be theoretically able to spend a greater part of the public resources on public goods. However, there could be two counter effects in this regard. A greater part of the public resources could be used for the private consumption of the ruling elite, or they might focus on those aspects of infrastructure that add prestige to the ruling elite. Bigger churches, museums, burial grounds, city squares, towers, avenues leading to the palaces could be part of this prestige-enhancing infrastructure. However, the urban traders and rural landlords might be putting some pressure on the ruling elite to control the expenditure for its own private goods consumption and prestige-enhancing infrastructure.

The former may like to have greater facilities in the form of ports, roads, etc. and more resources for the protection from those who are likely to capture their properties. What was actually provided as public goods under elite capture could be based on how these conflicting demands were resolved. However, there is no need to be surprised in seeing that a greater[2] amount of public goods is provided under elite capture.

Different Types of Elite Capture

There can be different forms of elite capture. For example, if we take India, the kingdoms ruled by local chieftains or those established by invaders from the territories which are currently part of India or elsewhere are all elite-captured states. The colonial government established by the British is part of such an invader state, but may have some special features compared to those established by other invaders. Moreover, even when democracy was formally established after Indian independence, there was a phase when the actual ruling was carried out by elites or those representing or acting on behalf of them at the national or state levels. Even today, it may not be uncommon to see (local) elites who have captured (and are ruling) local governments in different parts of India. We can consider these different forms of elite capture in the following paragraphs.

State by the Local Chieftains and Invaders

The state or its crude form starts with kinships or communities or extended families within which some common services are provided, where decision making on such services rest with certain people, and there are some return rewards to such decision

---

[2] 'Greater' is used here in the sense that it is more than what is demanded by the society as a whole or a median voter.

makers. 'Protection from enemies or outsiders' could be an important service (and hence, there is a public-goods role even for this crude form of government). The people who could compete well in providing 'protection' to own kinships/community/extended family would try to 'coerce' other communities or kinships to come under their protection. Hence, there is a territorial expansion of this 'protection' service, and that leads to invasion. (Of course, those invasions made just to plunder or rob resources of other territories and to return immediately back to one's territory are different. We are talking only about some form of states established by the invaders.) In that sense, the states by the local chieftains and by the invaders are different only in terms of the extent of expansion, and are not characteristically very different. Even a local chieftain may have extended his power over villages beyond his own.

The protection from robbers or other invaders could be the only form of public goods provided by such primitive rulers. In return, they might have received tax or rent from the (de facto or actual) property owners among the protected. There could be traders, and they too might be paying rent or tax to the rulers for the protection. This income might be used for the private (and limited public) goods consumption of the rulers.

Gradually, more established local kings or invaders who had expanded their territories substantially might have built more formal states providing a wider portfolio of public goods, including urban infrastructure (roads, water supply, drainage), limited educational and cultural organisations, and rural infrastructure (mainly irrigation), in addition to certain level of law and order and territorial protection. The protection of territory could have taken a major part of the state's resources because the ruler had a direct stake in this regard, and his military preparedness could be the only factor that discouraged potential invaders. (There were no other major factors that legitimised the sovereignty of a particular state then.) There would be tax or rent collection system, and the scope and reach of such systems varied considerably between different states ruled by elites. The acquisition of property owned or kept by others, including that of other kings or chieftains, was another option for enhancing the resources.

As the production systems in most of these cases were feudal, there were no major issues of state-mediating capitalist growth here. However, the manner in which chieftains dealt with early colonial traders could tell us something insightful in this regard. Either they collaborated with these traders in order to provide monopoly access to trade (different types of colonial traders—French, English, Dutch, etc.—fought amongst themselves to establish monopoly in colonial trade), or the local chieftains fought with (and most of the times got defeated by) colonialists due to the conflict in sharing the benefits over monopoly trade or to prevent what they considered as incursions into their zones of power. The latter process led to the emergence of colonial states. We will discuss these in detail next.

Colonialism as Elite Capture

A major part of the independent countries (or the members of United Nations today) were colonies for substantial periods (if we take the last four to five centuries). How do we see elite capture in such contexts? Some forms of kingdoms had existed in many parts of the world which were colonised by different foreign powers at different points of time. That would mean that (local) elite capture was operational in some of these countries even before the period of colonisation. We have discussed earlier that there could be 'business relations' between the local ruling elites and foreign traders, and the relationships with the potential colonisers might have started through this process. In any business relationship, the division of surplus between the parties depended on their respective bargaining power. An extreme form of the relationship is when one owns or captures the assets of the other. When the ruling elites want to get maximum surplus from the assets of the local or foreign capitalists, there could be nationalisation. On the other hand, when foreign traders want maximum surplus, there could be colonisation. Thus, business relationship between the ruling elites and foreign capitalists could manifest at any point in the spectrum marked by the extremes of colonisation and nationalisation.

Even when the foreign traders or capitalists established a rule overthrowing the local elite, it could only be another elite capture for the majority of the people within the country. Here, we could see different colonial rulers behaving differently in different countries. One could see a few strands in this regard. In case the colonialists had an interest in continuing to live in the colony, it could be an issue (Acemoglu et al., 2001). Here, the climate (and disease proneness) of the colony and the desperation of the early colonialists to find a new place for residence and economic investments might have mattered. The examples of US, Australia and New Zealand indicate this desperation as well as the favourable climate (Crosby, 1986). These might have encouraged the colonialists to build institutions (similar to their country of origin) in the 'new' world. In regions where long-term residence of the colonisers was found to be difficult, a much more arm-length ruling was conducted.

The second dimension could be the institutional character of the colonisers. It is argued that Britain with its common law tradition created a typical institutional structure in the colonies, whereas the colonisers from continental Europe had created another type of legal-institutional structure in the colonies (La Porta et al., 1998; North et al., 1998). How the colonisers mixed sexually with the people in the colonised world, or how the colonisers changed the ethnic composition of the population in the colonies could be yet another issue. In a number of Latin American colonies, the Spanish and Portuguese colonisers had mixed with local population and that created different incentives for the colonisers, and also different socio-cultural milieu.[3] The population brought in by the colonisers as workers (from Africa and Asia) and how they interacted with the local population could also be yet another factor.

In essence, colonial rule in most countries (other than those places where people from the colonial states see a prospect for long-term residence or converting them into own lands) witnessed a continuation of elite capture. However, the fact that they were

---

[3] The impact of ethno-linguistic fragmentation on development is discussed in Easterly and Levine (1997).

external rulers primarily interested in trade (as an input market for raw materials and an output market for their finished products) created some specific features in their governance. Just like other domestic elites, the colonial rulers too do not have the pressure to distribute private goods, in general, to the population at large. (In fact, the latter have much lesser pressure in this regard.) On the other hand, the fact that the colonial rulers from Europe had the exposure to a certain level of industrialisation (and modernisation later on) had some impact on the provision of certain goods and services. For example, although education is a part of private goods (but usually provided by the government, and has positive externalities for the society), the colonial rulers had greater incentive to provide such a service. The need to have educated people to handle their administrative tasks at the middle and lower levels could have driven their interest. Moreover, the fact that the colonialists came from relatively affluent societies might have also determined their ideas and norms on what are the desired level or nature of governmental provision of goods and services for a society; and these too have influenced such provision. Even the altruistic or religious organisations associated with the colonialists were interested in spreading education and healthcare to the people of the colonies, with whatever motives they had in this regard.

If institutions (such as law, judiciary and other regulatory institutions) can also be seen as part of public goods, the colonial rulers created the ones similar to their own world in the colonies. Through this process, certain advancement in terms of institutional evolution could be seen in the colonies. The public goods needs or the production possibilities, in this regard, of the colonisers were also advanced compared to the domestic rulers. For example, they might have realised the need for a sewerage system for a city and they were exposed to the then efficient technologies in this regard, and this might have influenced their decision on the provision of such a system in the colony. A similar picture could be seen in the provision of other governmental services under colonialism.

The governance of colonial rulers in terms of economic growth had some characteristics which were different from domestic rulers. First of all, colonial rulers and capitalists supported by them had a closer relationship. Hence, colonial rulers had lesser incentive to avoid monopoly practices in the colonies. Thus, the economic policies might have sustained the monopoly practices. The additional rent gained by the foreign companies might have gone out of the colonies, and the possible linkage effects that one could expect from the use of surplus for the expansion of domestic production might not have materialised. Thus, the criticism that colonialism did not enable the economic development of the colonies could be relevant in this regard (Bagchi, 1982).

When these colonies became independent, the governments in a major part of them were captured (or re-captured, if we notice the elite capture before the colonisation) by the domestic elites. If they became dictators under a domestic ruler or a section of the domestic elite, they sustained the features of elite capture as mentioned earlier. What if the exit of colonialism led to the establishment of formal democracy as in India?

Elite Capture under Democracy

It is possible that elite capture could sustain under democratic conditions. After the independence of India, the governments that came to exist immediately in a number of states in the country could be those controlled by local elites. The fact that the elections were conducted immediately after independence did not mean that electoral competition was intense then. It was possible for one party to have a dominant role in such a context. The Indian National Congress (INC) which had a leadership role in the freedom struggle had a dominating presence, whereas opposition parties were having only a minor presence in many states.

For elites to come to power through democracy, they need much more legitimacy than the fact that they are the elites. This could come from freedom struggles or due to economic, social and cultural factors. It could be that those elites who were part of the dominant party (or even the party itself could be insignificant, and it could be one or a few individuals) had multiple sources of legitimacy. They were reflecting the interests of the landlord class (and elite in terms of income or wealth because land was the major source of wealth then). They could also be at a higher position in terms of social hierarchy (probably due to their position in the caste system). Some of them had taken up leadership positions in the freedom struggle, giving them additional legitimacy to gather the support of the people at large. Or that they came from the educated sections of the society, and education in such contexts was a privilege of the few who were part of economic and social elites. Or it could be that there were no other reliable political mobilisations which could play a leadership role at that point of time.

Under such a situation of elite capture through democracy, the political power is by and large shared among a small section of elites in terms of wealth, education and social position. The majority of the population could be termed as somewhat 'blind' followers or vote banks. They could have multiple loyalties to the elites—as tenants or agricultural workers of the rural landlords, as followers of the caste hierarchy, as workers of the industrial or trade establishments, etc. Their voting decisions could be influenced greatly by a herd behaviour determined by the positions of the elites.

The distribution of private and public goods under a democratic elite capture could be somewhat different from that under a dictatorial elite capture. The public goods demand of the population at large could be at a lower level, as the private goods consumption is somewhat basic. However, there could be a greater need (or demand) for private goods distribution (resource transfer for private goods consumption) to the masses under a democratic system. Moreover, substantial sections of the population could not be excluded from such private goods distribution under a democracy (even though some groups could be excluded from such distribution under dictatorial regimes). Thus, the spending for private goods distribution could be higher under a democratic rule even if its basic character is that of elite capture.

A democratic rule would also mean greater integration of the urban and the rural through political process. The rural territories cannot be left unattended by the ruling elite. The rural landlords could be serving as agents of vote banks for the ruling elite.

Thus, there would be some transfer of resources between the ruling elites and rural landlords. This could be in the form of 'non-taxing' the rural elite (landlords) in return for their agency role in vote bank politics. There could be some provision of public goods in the rural areas aimed at rural elites. Expansion of irrigation could be one such case. In essence, the ruling elite had to share a greater amount of resources with the rural landlords in the democratic regime. This is primarily due to the need for support of the rural hinterlands at the time of elections (even when rural masses do not assert their individual rights much).

The public goods provision could be determined by the ruling elite and urban capitalists or traders (and we have already mentioned the need to transfer some resources to the rural landlords in this regard). However, elites operating under democracy are likely to have only a smaller share of resources for such public goods provision compared to that in a dictatorship. This is due to the greater need for transferring state resources for private goods consumption of the people at large. Probably, one can argue that an elite capture under democracy has lesser need to spend more money on military or police if the main purpose of that spending is the protection of the ruler from internal opposition. (Of course, such reduction in spending is unlikely if there is a continuing threat from foreigners or outsiders.) In one sense, there is a substitution between the military or police spending (for protection from internal opposition) and the spending for the private goods consumption of wider section of people. The latter may reduce the need for the former.

A similar impact could be seen in the use of public or state resource for own consumption of the ruling elite. It is obvious that there would be lesser restrictions on such consumption under dictatorship. However, some moderation in this regard could be seen on the part of the ruling elite under democracy. Such moderation might enhance the legitimacy of the rulers. There could be even extreme cases where the ruling elite does not take much state resources for personal consumption. This might make them very acceptable to the ruled. It is possible that some may capture the state or continue to rule it, not so much for enhancing personal consumption. There could be a trade-off between private consumption and the power that one derives through greater legitimacy. Thus, 'sacrificing' elite rulers need not be unusual. However, this need not change the 'elite capture' nature of the state in terms of governance.

The relationship between the capitalists and the ruling elite under democracy need not be characteristically different from that of dictatorship. Some specific groups of capitalists might establish closer relationship with the ruling elite, and this could have implications in terms of monopoly. There could be a bargaining between the capitalists and the ruling elites in terms of sharing the surplus, and here an extreme form of capturing the surplus (leading to nationalisation of the private enterprises) could also be an outcome. This depends on the relative power of the ruling elite and capitalists, and here whether the country is under democracy or dictatorship need not play an important role. This is mainly due to the fact that capitalists are less likely to be able to exercise control over the ruling elite through the democratic route.

Coming to the central issue of governance under elite capture, democracy may reduce the resources for public goods provision. This could have some impact on governance if public goods provision is to be an important part of this governance. Ruling elites could pursue growth-oriented policies if they desired to do so, as in the case of elites ruling under non-democratic situations. However, under democracy, such growth policies could not be harmful to large sections of society (say, by evacuating them from their land and so on). (If so, it could lead to the unsettling of the ruling elites in certain cases, which we would discuss in the next chapter.) Hence, there could be some minimal concern about making the economic growth palatable to wider sections of the society.

However, some level of discrimination might prevail in the provision of public services. The society would be divided between the elite and the non-elite, and the former would have privileged access to public services. Such privileged access may extend to the employment or private services provided by the state. This privileged access could also be used for sustenance of the rule of the democratically elected elite.

The possibility of having socially benevolent elite rulers who are interested in developing the country cannot be ruled out. They may want to make a long-lasting impact on the growth of the country. Or those elite rulers who see the need to contain possible threats to their rule may share public resources much more widely. Some of the middle-east countries could be examples in this regard. Such benevolent rulers may get a free hand under elite capture (and more so under dictatorship). From this point of view too, one need not be surprised if regimes captured by elites facilitate significant economic growth. Benevolent elite rulers may also use this growth to build domestic human and technological capacities for production.

Corruption and Elite Capture

Before analysing the nature of corruption under elite capture, we need to understand what we mean by corruption, and this is discussed in Box 2.1.

Box 2.1:
Understanding Corruption

There can be a legal understanding of corruption. This is when some people who are supposed to observe or enforce an existing law or rule try to circumvent it intentionally with or without paying or taking a bribe or other favours. Paying and/or taking a bribe could be privately beneficial. There is corruption in not enforcing the law where it should be enforced, and this is the most notable form of corruption. There is corruption in enforcing (or threatening to enforce) the law where it should not be enforced. Not taking a decision or an action clearly and timely on the basis of an existing rule could also be harmful for some (especially for those who follow the rule). People may try to circumvent this through corruption. People may pay a bribe when some action which is supposed to be taken in due course is taken at a pace faster than normal.

However, an economic understanding of corruption could be slightly different. It should start by analysing whether the law or rule (which is

(Box 2.1 contd)

(Box 2.1 contd)

circumvented by the people through corruption) is efficient or not. If the law or rule is inefficient, and not having the law or rule is more efficient than having it, then not enforcing the rule (with or without corruption) need not be socially harmful. For example, if there is a restriction on imports which is causing reduction in social welfare (through the losses suffered by the consumers which are greater than the gains made by the domestic producers), its non-enforcement (with or without corruption) would create less harm than its rigorous enforcement. However, there can be some social losses here if there is corruption (and hence, its non-enforcement). This is due to the diversion of socially useful resources for what is called rent-seeking. When somebody imposes a restriction on import (by the enforcement of a rule) and, hence, someone else gains (due to the limited competition by disallowing imports), the former may get rent (a share of the extra profit made by the latter). This may encourage many others to seek such rents. Thus, they may indulge in such rent-seeking activities, diverting resource from directly useful productive activities.

The existence of a law need not be the only constraint that somebody wants to overcome through corruption. Whenever there are institutional constraints that limit surplus creation for the individual or groups or organisations, they may try to take steps to avoid such constraints. However, certain institutional constraints (including law) are useful even when it limits surplus creation for some individuals because the surplus created by them may cause greater loss for the society. For example, a polluting firm may create surplus by circumventing the law controlling pollution, but this pollution causes a loss to the society greater than the additional gains made by the polluter. Thus, corruption is socially harmful if it leads to surplus creation for some, but that causes greater social loss.

What is the role of corruption in the context of mutually beneficial transactions? There are many situations where institutions (including law) would debilitate mutually beneficial transactions (even those which do not create a negative externality, such as pollution). A law which bans selling of agricultural land to a non-agricultural activity could be one such constraint. In this particular case, such a law is not reducing any social loss. This is so because laws or institutions need not always come to exist to avoid social losses. Or even when these come to exist with the purpose of reducing social loss, it may become irrelevant after some time, but may continue to exist due to the difficulties

(Box 2.1 contd)

(Box 2.1 contd)

> in changing them. Laws/norms/other institutions once made, require
> substantial effort to change them. Hence, there can be corruption to
> overcome institutional constraints that prevent mutually beneficial
> exchanges. However, this corruption cannot be reckoned economically
> harmful, except for its effect on encouraging rent-seeking activities and
> diversion of efforts towards socially unproductive activities.
>
> *Source:* Author.

Elites, due to historical property rights or their current control over government, are likely to have greater command over
resources or public resources. Elites may corner or access public
resources without much corruption in a legal sense. This is so
because they can design the laws (and create norms) in such way
that their access to public resources for their personal benefits or
for the public goods needed by them are made legal or legitimate.
Hence, one could see spending of substantial amount of resources
for the needs of the elite rulers or for their amenities without the
society considering it as illegal or corrupt.

If disallowing mutually beneficial transactions or allowing it
only on giving bribe is reckoned as corruption in an economic sense,
the incentives of the elites could be somewhat different. Sections
of elites or their close allies of domestic or foreign investors were
those who participated in these mutually beneficial exchanges.
Hence, they had an incentive to facilitate such exchanges. This
could be an incentive to minimise corruption in one sense. They
did not have to take bribes in allowing such mutually beneficial
exchanges, as they themselves were (one of) the beneficiaries such
exchanges. For example, think about the opportunity to develop
a natural resource (such as ores) within the country. A foreign or
a domestic capitalist may be interested in developing it. If the law
(or the informal rule) does not allow such development and this
rule can be circumvented only by paying a bribe to the ruler, there
is corruption in an economic sense. However, under elite capture,
this need not happen. The ruling elite could be the de-facto owner
of the natural resources due to historical property rights, which

are preserved through elite capture or due to their current control of the resource as the ruler. Thus, the elite ruler or owner and the industrialist may enter into a mutually beneficial transaction through sharing of the surplus. Thus, the surplus generating activity may take place without much corruption, which reduces the scope of such mutually beneficial exchange.

However, the elite rulers do not have the incentive to bring in competition in the economic activities, since they could be part or joint owners of the enterprises or direct beneficiaries of the profits enjoyed by the opportunities of monopolistic behaviour. Thus, if we reckon the continuation of social loss associated with monopoly due to the collusion between the government and industry as a form of corruption, this is more likely to persist under elite capture.

Another form of corruption is in those cases where people use bribes to avoid the enforcement of rules instituted for public purposes. In situations of elite capture, the public purpose rules were generally made to meet the relevant needs of the elites, as the income status of the majority was at a very low level and, hence, the demand for public goods from them would also be insignificant. Then elite rulers could make public purpose rules to meet their needs, and not for the public at large. Hence, they have greater incentives to enforce the rules made to serve their own public goods needs (or purposes). These could include better roads, disciplined traffic, better waste collection, quality water supply, reliable electricity supply, better policing and rule of law, and so on in the urban territories where the ruling and other elites live. Thus, it should not be surprising to see some of the public amenities or facilities working relatively well (in the limited urban territories) under elite capture.

Under elite capture, corruption was likely to be centralised. This was so because the elites do not have to redistribute much wealth or money to others. Hence, they need not allow decentralised corruption. If central rulers become indifferent to the corruption of the lower level functionaries of the government, it could be the part of an implicit redistribution strategy to make a section of support base happy. The pressure to do so is minimal under elite capture. Hence, elite capture could, in certain cases, impose a system of governance that is forced to deliver without allowing the lower tiers of the bureaucracy to tax people through widespread corruption.

Media and Elite Capture

Media[4] plays an important role in bringing out the failures of the government into public domain, and hence it helps moving towards better governance. Amartya Sen has shown the importance of media in encouraging effective actions during the famines (Sen & Dreze, 1989). The role of media in terms of governance under elite capture is the focus of this section. However, it is useful to understand, as a prelude, certain economic and political economy features of media, and these are discussed briefly in Box 2.2.

Information circulation is needed for all types of rulers. Even for a dictator, there is a certain need for legitimisation, and this requires some information to be provided to the ruled. Hence, elite-captured governments too would support or sustain some form of media. However, it is most likely that in such cases the media firms are owned by either the government controlled by elite or some other section of elites. Even if there are multiple channels of media and they compete, it could be that between firms owned by different sections of elite (who are part of the ruling class).

If such elite-ruled societies have a majority who are poor or with very low incomes, the subscription of the media among these sections could be very limited. In that case, not only the ownership of the media rests with the elite, but most of the readers would also come from the elite sections. Hence, the media would attempt to cover the issues of interest to them. There is no need for the media to extend the coverage of issues of interest to the others, since they

---

[4] It includes print newspapers, TV and magazines of different types owned by different stakeholders, such as government, private companies, political parties and civil society organisations. Media also includes other forms of informal information circulation by interest groups. During these days, internet and online sources, including social network sites, play an important role in providing information to the public at large.

Box 2.2:
Economics and Political Economy of the Media

Media is expected to provide information. This information provision has some 'public goods' features—it is difficult to exclude somebody from consuming it, and it is also indivisible. Hence, it is very difficult to exclude the non-payer who reads or uses this information, and this poses some problems in organising information provision as a private enterprise. Even though the subscriber of a newspaper pays, all readers of a newspaper cannot be made to pay. It looks that such information provision or the primitive forms of media were not seen as commercial ventures in the beginning, even though they may have recovered the cost of production through subscription or other means. This could be due to the inherent problem of information supply mentioned here.

In some cases, the government owns the media, which is useful to address the 'public goods' nature of information supply. However, when the government owns the media, its interest may influence the contents of the media. It is very likely that the government-controlled media represents the interests of the rulers. Moreover, government-controlled media do not have the incentives to generate adequate revenue, and hence they do not have to meet the needs of the customers. Thus, they are less likely to produce what is demanded or needed by the subscribers. The fact that the survival of the government-controlled media does not depend on its acceptance by the subscribers will have an impact on its efficiency and usefulness or acceptance.

When the media is controlled by the private firm (or when the media is an independent company), it is expected to make a profit from the subscription charges and advertisement revenue. In those cases where a media functions as part of a multiproduct firm, there can be some cross-subsidy if the media helps the firm in other ways—say, to exercise some political control so as to benefit other businesses. In other cases where the main product or service is the media, profit from this service is important. Or consistent losses may lead to the closing down of its operations. Hence, it is likely to meet the demands of those sections of the society which can subscribe it and/or which can enhance the advertisement revenue. Such enhancement of advertisement revenue is possible only when more among the subscribers are, or could become, the consumers of the advertised products and services. Advertisers' willingness to pay for the space in a particular media depends on the number as well as the spending ability of its subscribers or readers. Thus, there is a relationship between the subscription and advertisement revenue, or that these two are not completely independent. Hence, the media is likely to concentrate on the subscribers and potential consumers of advertised products and services.

(Box 2.2 contd)

(Box 2.2 contd)

If the media firms' objective is to maximise profit, there could be a selection of consumers that maximise the profit. The type of these consumers may vary from one society to another depending on the economy and the spread of income. Thus, the media may concentrate on the issues of the elites in a society when only those elites can subscribe the media, and can become the major consumers of the commercial products and services. On the other hand, media starts focussing on a wider section of the society, as more and more people join the club of subscribers and consumers. Then there could be a situation in which different media firms may focus on different sets of consumers.

Media is a product for which no society can depend solely on imports (say, from foreign sources). The local language media is non-tradable, such as housing or nursing care. One cannot import such non-tradable goods or services from elsewhere, and these have to be produced within each context. Hence there will be local media, even if the cost of production goes up, since the demand for local-language media cannot be met through imports. Thus, one can see investments in media production, even if capitalists do not want to invest in manufacturing of other tradable commodities due to cost disadvantages (and where people depend on products brought in from somewhere else).

There are also economies of scale in the functioning of media. The per-unit cost of supplying a media product is likely to come down as more of it is produced. It is the cost of information collection and organisation that have the economy of scale in the production of newspapers and TV channels. The marginal cost of a newspaper would come down drastically to the cost of the newsprint used in each copy of the paper. This is so because the additional cost of information collection and organisation per copy may become negligible as more and more copies are produced. There are increasing returns to scale in advertisement revenue too. The price that the advertiser would be willing to pay per unit space of the newspaper (or unit time of TV) would be increasing as the subscriber base is widening (and also based on their average per-capita income). Hence, this can give incentives for some consolidation in the media industry. The media with higher levels of circulation can also improve its quality of presentation or its appeal to the readers. This may also include the coverage of information. Hence, there could be some 'demand externality' too operating in the case of media—the process by which there would be greater incentive for a consumer to use a product as there are more and more consumers using the same product.

Source: Author.

cannot afford to be the subscribers. Some of the accounts of poor and vulnerable may appear in the media to satisfy the demand for such stories of human interest of the elite.

The collaboration between the capitalists and the rulers need not be a major issue for the media under such elite capture. However, this can become an issue if there is a conflict among the sections of ruling elites and these contesting parties have some control over media. There could be strategic collaboration between the external or foreign powers and those sections of the elite that are unhappy with the government. There would be an expansion of the supply of contested information in such a setting, and this is an important step towards political competition between elites in these societies.

However, since media is in the business of ideas and public discourses, it would be wrong to assume that the ideas circulated by the media within a society are driven fully by endogenous factors. Hence, when the world is divided between the developed and undeveloped, modern and pre-modern, democratic and non-democratic, it is always possible to have some circulations of the ideas of modernity, development and democracy even in an undeveloped, pre-modern and dictatorial setting.

As frustration gathers momentum among the non-elites or certain other sections of the elite about the government, there could be a beginning of the circulation of counter-media there. The circulation of small magazines, pamphlets, booklets and so on may gradually catch up, provided the government is not bent upon censoring all forms of counter-media. What is important for us is to note that even without such dictatorship (and censorship), and even with competition between different media firms, one should not expect a penetration of the media among the ruled or a concern about the issues of the ruled among the media under elite capture.

What Is Wrong with Elite Capture?

We have argued that there is nothing inevitable that leads to the slowdown of economic growth under elite capture. There could be a higher level of the provision of public goods, even though there could be privileged access to public services for some sections of the society. What is wrong with this situation?

There are two ways of analysing this question. The first is to know whether such a situation is efficient (within the framework of economics) without bothering about the distribution of gains and wealth in such societies. There could be some reasons which make such situations inefficient even if there is economic growth. We have said that there could be higher economic growth and provision of public goods under elite capture, but this is not certain. It depends to a great extent on the nature of the elites. When a fewer number of people are the decision makers, even the irrationality or the idiosyncrasies of these individuals could make a difference in the outcome. Hence, even if the situation provided incentives to usher in economic growth or public goods provision, these need not be internalised by those rulers in such circumstances. The lack of adequate competition would not create a situation where inefficient rulers are superseded by the efficient ones. The elite capture, especially that under non-democratic situations, does not provide enough opportunities to correct the 'rulers' who might deviate from rational or efficient decisions. (This can happen only by overthrowing them. This possibility is discussed in the next section.) Thus, the expected benefits from elite capture need not be actually derived under all such contexts.

Elite capture could lead to a distribution of a greater part of the surplus (generated through economic growth) among the few, and the wider sections of society may get nothing or little. The reversal of this situation would require an assertion of the power of non-elites, and this has to be resisted for the sustenance of elite capture. The skewed nature of the distribution of surplus and wealth would mean that the majority of the society could encounter problems in accessing assets, such as capital or education for enhancing their incomes. Thus, as noted in the literature of economics of under-development, such societies may have only a limited domestic market for products and a limited pool of entrepreneurs and skilled personal, and this may limit the growth potential of that country.[5] Hence, the skewed distribution of surplus itself may create an inefficient situation there.

Another way of analysing the undesirability of elite capture is that even if it leads to economic growth and the provision of public goods, the situation may not be liked by the majority of the people there. Hence, the elite capture is not a sustainable equilibrium. This is so irrespective of whether the country is democratic or under dictatorship. The non-elites who see unequal distribution of public resources, surpluses from the production systems, and also power would demand a greater part of the cake. This could take place, gradually and relatively, peacefully under democratic regimes. But it could take place (probably spontaneously and violently) in non-democratic situations. Under dictatorship, the ruling elites would have to spend greater and greater amount of resources to protect themselves from those who may try to unsettle them. This spending for self-protection of the elites could become unsustainable over a period of time.

Hence, even if there is economic growth and adequate provision of public goods, elite capture would be undesirable for the majority of the people over a period of time. Hence, a change in elite capture is somewhat inevitable. The change might be socially efficient if we consider such social efficiency as the one determined by the aggregation of the welfare of the majority of the people there. Even if it is not efficient, such a change is somewhat inevitable. Hence, anybody interested in good governance needs to think beyond elite capture, even if the ruling elites are growth oriented and are concerned about providing 'good governance'.

An Empirical Note on Elite Capture

We have talked about the features of elite capture so far without referring to many real-world examples. This approach is used here since the purpose of this book is to develop a consistent theoretical

---

[5] Imperfections in capital markets leading to the underinvestment of the poor and its impact growth is discussed in Banerjee and Newman (1993).

story. Moreover, it does not intend to give exhaustive empirical material as that may require rewriting (or copying) the histories of all nations once again. Hence, only a few examples are highlighted here. Examples of elite capture are numerous in the world. Almost all the regimes in the world before the eighteenth century had some or other feature of elite capture. Most parts of the world ruled by chieftains, kings and so on are clear examples of elite capture. As discussed earlier, the colonial rules can also be viewed as one form of elite capture. There were many cases where the ruling elite was moderated or restrained by other sections of elite through very limited democratic process. The Council of Tenants-in-Chief introduced in 1066 AD in England, represented by the feudal landlords and the clergy, advising the king could be an early example of such moderation. This had also led to the Magna Carta in 1215 AD with more institutionalised restrictions on the king. Most of the conflicts, between the ruling elites and other sections of elite, including the English Civil War in the seventeenth century were to control the excessive and personalised expenditures of the kings. The constitutional monarchy that came to exist in England could be the first example where the elite-captured state started undergoing transformation based on pressures from others— probably sections of elite who control the economy or trade. Despite the functioning of some form of Parliament in Britain for most of the period of the second millennium (AD), actual participation in this democratic process was limited to not more than 3 per cent of adult male population until the eighteenth century. Hence, this democracy itself was elitist. There are similar examples in continental Europe, especially North-west Europe. The city-based merchants had a greater say in the ruling of the Dutch city-states. The regimes before the French Revolution in West Europe could be called elite-captured ones.[6]

The situation in America was a little different. The early colonialists of North America or specifically the United States were not part of the elites of the motherland, and that could be a reason for an early transition to democracy there. In fact, there was an elitist

---

[6] For a description of the changes in France, see Magraw (1983).

basis in the American Civil War wherein the southern confederacy (which had the moral support of the elite sections in Britain) with their insistence on the continuation of slavery—representing an elite position. But this could be suppressed by the relatively more democratic and modern northerners within the United States, who built the early form of democracy within the country. Most of the pre-colonial and colonial rules in Africa and Asia were elite-captured states as far as the colonised are concerned. The Spanish colonies in Latin America were elite-captured states until the eighteenth century. Haiti could be one country where elite capture ended early due to the overthrowing of the (French) colonialists by the black worker population brought by them.[7]

Even after independence, elite capture continued for a number of decades in the then newly independent countries, such as India, due to the lack of deepening of democracy. One party or one ruler could continue in power without much real opposition in many such countries. These periods were also of elite capture. Thus, the period during which the INC could continue in power without effective opposition in the central government or in state governments can be reckoned as that of elite capture. The elites came to power in Pakistan immediately after its independence. This was followed by series of military capture of power, and that could be another form of elite capture. Elites of Pakistan ruled the area which is currently known as Bangladesh for about three decades. Even after independence, there were periods of limited democracy and elite capture in Bangladesh. Although Pakistan and Bangladesh currently show a deepening of democracy, most of the leadership of the competing parties comes from elite sections. Although there has been emergence of leaders from non-elite sections in India as a whole, there are local governments in many states in India, such as UP, which continued to have features of elite capture even in the eighties and nineties (Lieten, 1996). Elites have ruled in collaboration with the kingdom in Nepal until recently. Bhutan has moved to limited democracy only recently. However, Sri Lanka

---

[7] For Haiti, see Lundahl (1983).

had shown signs of deepening democracy relatively quickly after independence, even though it got into ethnic tussle afterwards.

There were many countries where some sections of non-elites captured power from the state, but over a period of time these non-elites became elites and they controlled the state. Iraq, Libya and many other African countries are examples in this regard. Although there were non-elite routes for the formation of the governments there, they showed features similar to elite capture over a period of time.

Threats to the Elites

The threats to elites could come from different sources. It could arise from the disgruntled or frustrated elements within the elite. The ambitious chiefs of the army could be another source of threat. If the regime is non-democratic, the credibility of the threat requires support from sections of the military or other armed gangs. Thus, some insiders (part of ruling elite including its military generals) also could threaten the ruling elite. Hence, it would be possible to see a regime of elite thrown out by some other elements of the same elite. Such overthrowing is not uncommon in elite rules. While talking about elite capture in this chapter, we do not presume that the same ruler (or sub-group) would continue to be in power all the time. There could be regime changes as part of the succession and (violent and non-violent) competition among the members of the same elite. However, this does not change the elite-capture nature of the government. Thus, whatever we have mentioned here as the characteristics of elite-captured state are relevant even if there are changes in the specific elites holding state power. There could also be threats coming from foreign powers. This might in some cases lead to the establishment of new elite rulers within the country (who collaborate with the foreigners) or of foreign rule. However, these too do not change the basic (elite-capture) nature of this state, as far as governance in concerned.

However, much more interesting for us are the situations wherein the elites (who hold state power) encounter opposition from sections of non-elites. Severe disenchantment with the ruling regime might lead to popular uprising against the ruling elites. There could be two major types of popular mobilisation. First could come from specific social/ethnic/regional/religious groups who perceive a long period of marginalisation or exclusion by the ruling elites. Blacks struggling against White rulers or lower caste uprising against upper-caste rulers or Muslim uprising against Hindu or Christian rulers are examples of this kind. There are innumerable cases of such assertions against rulers from all over the world. Here, the difference in the social identity between the ruled and the ruler is the prime issue for mobilisation.

Secondly, there could be a class-based uprising against the ruling elite. What had occurred in most of the socialist countries was a manifestation of this class-based threat to the ruling elites. Here, the rulers and the ruled may be sharing the same social identity, of say, Orthodox Christianity or Slavic ethnicity as in the case of Russia. The mobilisation of the underclass could be on the basis of a combination of economic factors (such as their quality of life could be distinctly inferior to that of the ruling elite and the capitalist class) and ideologies.

In both these cases (that is, social-based or class-based threats to the ruling elite), success would depend on group or political mobilisation and the leadership. Hence, the identity-based marginalisation or class-based exploitation need not lead to an explicit form of uprising in the absence of such mobilisation and leadership. There could be personal qualities of the leadership, ideas and ideologies rationalising or legitimising such uprisings. Sometimes it would be difficult to isolate the ideological and material factors behind the uprisings, and there could be a symbiotic relationship between these two.

We will consider the capture of the state by these counter-elites (social group and the under-class) and its impact on governance in the following chapters.

3

Capture of Governments by Social Counter-Elites

When some people feel alienated from the state captured by the elite, one response could be an assertion of these people based on their different social identities, that is, religion, race, ethnicity, caste, region. Obviously, such assertion is possible only if the ruling elite and displeased sections of the ruled have different social identities. Such an assertion is less likely in relatively homogenous societies where most share similar religious, ethnic, racial identities. Even if there is discontent among some sections of society, their assertion is less likely to be successful if they are only a very small minority or when such people are scattered around different parts of the country.

We have already mentioned the identities or groups of people who may constitute these social counter-elites. These include a specific race, caste, religion, ethnic group or people living in a sub-region who share some aspects of identity and a feeling that the ruling elite does not represent them. Some of these identities, such as religion, are changeable but others are not. A particular social identity may represent the marginalised in one context, whereas the same could be the dominant one in another context. Religions, such as Judaism, Christianity, Islam and Hinduism represent the marginalised groups in certain situations even when these are the identities of the ruling elites in certain other contexts.

It could be that one such group feels an explicit marginalisation by the state in a situation or that the people who share the feeling of such marginalisation may happen to share the same social identity.

In rare cases, people who perceive marginalisation may create a common social identity—say, by converting into one religion. In those cases, a homogenous identity is created after the perceived marginalisation, but in most cases it is perceived as an outcome of their identity different from that of the ruling elites.

In certain situations, some of these marginalised social groups are able to capture power from the ruling elites. Such capturing can be through democratic or non-democratic means. If the marginalised social group is the majority and their identity is distinct from the ruling elite, then the capture by these non-elites is relatively easier either through democracy or through the violent or non-violent overthrowing of the prevailing regime through non-democratic ways. To some extent, the success of the independence struggles can be seen as a part of such non-elite capture when we see foreign rulers as the elites with a different social identity. Here, national identity becomes the mobilising slogan for capturing the state from foreign elites. Even in those cases where the ruling elites are from within the country but are viewed inadequately nationalistic, there can be mobilisations on the basis of nationalism. Hence, such nationalist capture of the state can also be counted as part of social counter-elite captures. However, the people who capture the state on the basis of nationalist slogans can also be elites who were not part of the previous rulers.

There can be different layers of counter-elites. For example, in the context where a country is ruled by the elites from the dominant social group, the marginalised social groups may be driving the counter-elite capture. However, there could be a small section of elite even among the marginalised social groups, and they may be leading the counter-elite mobilisation and the capture. Or if there were no such elites, it could be possible to have the emergence of an elite section in due course in these marginalised groups which capture the state. There could be opposition to these new elites who control the state, and it can lead to another counter-elite capture. Hence, counter-elite capture need not be seen as leading to the disappearance of the elite capture forever, but there could be repetitions of elite and counter-elite captures. But this would eventually lead to greater democratisation, and, as we see in the following paragraphs, a widening of the distribution of public resources to the majority.

It is possible to see some sections of non-elite capturing the state even when they are not the majority. Some divisions among the other sections of people could bring in a particular minority group into power. This could also be due to superior armed (or violent) power with or without the help of external forces. One could see regimes formed by minority social groups propped up or supported by foreign powers. An extreme form of this is the foreign rule itself which is legitimised in the name of supporting the oppressed minorities. One can also see formal or informal coalitions among different non-elite social groups leading to the capture of the state through democracy.

There could be some cases where people at large or a substantial section of the ruled support military takeover when the elites who ruled (either as part of a formal democracy or as dictators) were seen as ineffective or socially harmful. (This is slightly different from the transition wherein one elite dictator is replaced by another one—possibly from the army.) There are some elements of counter-elite capture here if the power gets transferred from the disliked or unpredictable ruler to a rule-bound regime. However, such military takeovers need not necessarily lead to the changes in the allocation of public resources that we will discuss in the following sections.

Impacts of Social Counter-Elite Capture

One need not expect structural changes like the decline of feudalism as part of social counter-elite capture. This is so because there could be cases where landlords and tenants (and agricultural workers) share the same identity (say that of a religion or region), and their joint capture of the state through a struggle based on this identity is less likely to work against these landlords. Instead, it could be that these landlords have played a leadership role in this counter-elite capture, enabling the continuation of their dominant role after the state capture.

Provision of Private Goods

Since the driving force behind the counter-elite capture is the perceived marginalisation, it is reasonable to assume that a substantial section of the people representing such group belongs to the poor or economically vulnerable sections. These sections would not have benefitted much from the limited distribution of private goods under the elite capture. This could be one important reason for, or the manifestation of, the perceived marginalisation. Hence, there would be pressures on the counter-elites who capture the state to enhance the distribution of private goods (including transfer of public resources for private consumption) to these sections of society. This has two impacts: the coverage of private goods distribution goes up in such contexts, and, secondly, the share of public resources needed for such private goods distribution (or transfer) would increase.

We have argued that under elite-capture, a substantial part of the burden of public goods distribution or individual welfare (such as the support needed for an unemployed or an aged worker) was more likely borne by the smaller units of the ruled, such as family, kinships, communities, landlord and people working them, and so on. However, as a part of the counter-elite capture, some part of this burden could be taken over by, or transferred to, the state. This could happen because it was with the active support and participation of some of these 'ruled' units that the counter-elites came to power. Hence, counter-elite capture inevitably leads to certain expansion of the government in terms of its actual reach among the citizens.

The counter-elites who capture the state may also try to enhance the kitty of public resources. Imposing higher taxes on the incomes of previously ruled elites, and affluent sections and capitalists who colluded or associated with these elites could be one such source for additional revenue. There could be higher taxes on private consumption itself through indirect taxes. New rulers would be willing to do so since this might not affect their support base, as their level of consumption could be lower. There could also be a capturing of part of the resources or assets held by the elites and capitalists. In extreme cases, there could be nationalisation of private firms owned by the capitalists or elites. All these strategies could be used by the counter-elites who capture the state to enhance the quantum of public money. They needed more money to meet the distribution of private goods in the society.

Provision of Public Goods

The impact of the capture of state by social counter-elites on the provision of public goods may depend on a number of factors. If the increased demand for the distribution of private goods to a larger section of society could be met only with a greater share of public resources (compared to the situation under elite capture) even after the efforts to enhance such resources, it could have a negative impact on the provision of public goods. Hence, the quantum of pubic goods provision could go down as part of counter-elite capture in relative terms or, in certain cases, in absolute terms. This might affect the affluent sections because it is they who have a higher demand for such public goods. (Here, too, we assume a positive relationship between the demand for public goods in general and income or wealth status.) It may also affect the capitalists or industrialists, as they would also need a higher level of public goods, such as infrastructure for their economic activities.

If the counter-elites and their support base as a whole were having a wealth or income status inferior to the previously ruling elite, then the demand for public goods by the former could be at a lower level. Hence, even if there was a reduction in the provision of public goods as part of the counter-elite capture, it might not bother these new rulers or their support base much. However, the demand for public goods by all sections of counter-elites capturing the state or supporting them need not be low. For example, if culti-vating classes are part of this group, they may demand irrigation[1] or rural roads. Under such cases, there could be an expansion of irrigation to a larger section without charging them or by giving more money to individuals to acquire irrigation through private means (say through bore wells). If education was previously accessible mainly to the elites, and if education is valued by the counter-elites or their support base, there could be an expansion of this service. (Education is not a public good in the strict sense, but expansion of education has positive externalities, and it is a pub-licly provided service in many countries.) There could be similar goods and services whose provision may expand under counter-elite capture. Even if the quantum of provision is not expanding, there could be an effort to enhance the access to such services. This could even lead to a reduction in the per capita availability of such services available to the affluent sections. Hence, electricity could be made accessible to a larger section of people even when there is not enough increase in its generation. If there were some pricing of such publicly provided services under elite capture, there would be pressures to subsidise them to sections of consumers as part of the counter-elite capture.

We have seen that the protection to the capitalists or traders and other members of the propertied class was one public good pro-vided under elite capture. However, the counter-elites capturing the state need not be that committed at least in the initial phase to give the same level of protection to these sections. There could be some nationalisation, and it is one form of infringement on private

---

[1] Strictly speaking, irrigation is not a pure public good. It is divisible, as one person's use reduces the quantum of water available for the other, but the cost of excluding somebody from using surface irrigation (say, canal water) is costly.

property. In fact, the property rights of the previous elites may not be seen as a right itself requiring protection. However, this position may change if the counter-elites themselves support a set of capitalists who collaborate with them, or if the rulers see the lack of property rights as a reason for the decline of capital investments there, or when some of these counter-elites are or emerge as a part of the propertied class.

Counter-Elite Capture through Democracy

There could be some differences in the nature of counter-elite capture depending on whether it comes to power through formal democracy or not. We have seen that elite capture through formal democracy may lead to a greater distribution of private goods compared to that in dictatorship. Hence, there is a certain impact of democracy itself even if the rule can be called elite capture. A similar situation could be there under counter-elite capture too. This is so because counter-elites come to power in a democratic situation through competing with elites. Competitive democracy has certain inherent advantages (for which we will devote a full chapter later), and these will start reflecting even in a context where the state is captured by counter-elites through elections. Democracy gives more reliable information on the breeding of opposition to the rulers, compared to a situation where there were no elections. In the latter case, the growing opposition to the government may come as a surprise to the rulers. The 'superior information' under democracy may encourage them to do something to mitigate the negative feelings of the ruled, and hence it may lead to a greater diversion of the public resources from the elites to the ruled (more likely for private goods.) The counter-elite who capture the state in the context of formal democracy also have similar incentives. Thus, they may give more resources (here, again, most likely for private goods) not only to their own non-elite social group, but also to other such groups.

Governance under Counter-Elite Capture

Counter-elites have seen that the elites were using state power in the past to get privileged access to private and public goods, and services. Hence, for the new rulers, an assertion of their rights after capturing the state would mean a similarly privileged access to state-provided goods and services for themselves, and also for their support base. Therefore, one might see tendencies like the distribution of government positions to members of one's own group and supporters (without much consideration of merit or abilities) under counter-elite capture. One should not expect an improvement in governance, if we mean by that an across-the-board improvement in public service delivery or distribution by considering the 'eligibility' unrelated to the closeness of the citizen with the rulers. However, if the ruling counter-elite represents the majority or a wider section of the society (compared to the previously ruling elite), then a distribution of privileges associated with state power may actually lead to the distribution to a wider society. Or they may be forced to use some 'neutral' or 'unbiased' criteria to distribute the 'privileges', as there are too many people and too fewer positions or too much demand and very limited resources. This expansion of the coverage of distribution of the state privileges itself could be a progressive step.

However, the fact that the section of counter-elites which has captured the state is formed on the basis of one social identity (caste, race, religion, sub-region, ethnicity, etc.), and their struggle against the previously ruled elite was based on the identity of that group would have some impact on the coverage of state privileges. There is some likelihood of the decline of the state privileges of the social group closely aligned with the previously ruling elite. This is especially so, if the latter could not amass wealth that cannot be captured by the new rulers. Similarly, other social groups which have not collaborated with the state-capturing group may not see much improvement in their access to state-provided services or privileges. Thus, there can be an identity-based expansion of the coverage of the state-provided private goods and employment under the state ruled by social counter-elites.

Capitalist Investments under Counter-Elite Rulers

The relationship between the social counter-elites who have captured the state and capitalists is also an interesting issue. There could be a negative impact on those set of capitalists who were having a cosy (or crony) relationship with the previously ruling elite, unless they showed acumen in shifting their allegiance just before or immediately after the collapse of the elite-ruled state. We have argued earlier that it is possible to see some 'nationalisation' or the state-capture of the resources held by the capitalists who were loyal to the elite rulers. The notion of power internalised by the counter-elite could also be one of developing a close (crony) relationship with specific capitalists. The social counter-elite may visualise the need for a wealth-creating class (unlike class-based counter-elites that we will discuss in the next chapter). Hence, they too would be interested in cultivating such relationship with the existing capitalists who have shifted loyalty or the newer ones from within or outside the country. There are two kinds of expectation from these collaborating capitalists. First is to create wealth, create employment and to contribute to the public (tax) resources of the state. Second is a contribution to the private resources of the rulers. (These expectations are not very different from the case of an elite ruler or even some of the advanced forms of government.) The second expectation would lead to some granting of the monopoly power to the capitalists, and this is a source of crony capitalism. (This would be changed only when there is a social constituency which suffers from monopoly, that is, lack of competition in commodity or factor markets. We will discuss this issue in Chapter 6.)

Corruption under Social Counter-Elite Capture

The incentives for (controlling) corruption under counter-elite capture can be understood in comparison with elite capture. The leaders of counter-elite capture are less likely to come from economic elites. Thus, they may demand more (public) resources even for their private consumption. Moreover, they may need resources to distribute among the sections of society which helped them to capture power. The need for such redistribution is much more crucial for the counter-elites as compared to the elites. Hence, counter-elite rulers are likely to capture a greater part of the public resources. Some of these could manifest as corruption in both legal and economic terms.

We are not taking a moral view here. It could be that the economic elites had historically enjoyed greater access to resources, and some parts of this history could be very extractive or exploitative. Moreover, the legal system is likely to legitimise such historically acquired assets and access to resources. Hence, elites may have lesser needs to meet their private consumption through public resource in the way it is constructed. Such use can be interpreted as corruption in legal terms. Thus, the elites may be seen as less corrupt in legal or common sense terms.

Counter-elite capture is to be seen as part of redistribution of assets or endowments in society. Whether such redistribution leads to more resources for the leadership of counter-elites or for the people at large is a moot question. Such changes in the regimes of governance will lead to redistribution of resources even when there is no formal or legal redistribution, such as land reforms in a country. Hence, the acquisition of a greater share of the public resources, if it happens under counter-elite capture, can also be taken as part of a dynamic redistribution happening in society.

How does this redistribution shape corruption in an economic sense? This depends on the means by which counter-elites corner greater parts of public resources. If their government imposes a greater amount of (lump sum) tax on some sections of society, and this additional resource is distributed (through cash transfer) among another section of society, then there could be minimum social losses or economic corruption. There could be some loss due to the diversion of productive effort to corner a greater part of redistributed wealth, and also to avoid such imposition of taxes.

However, such window of efficient redistribution may not exist for the counter-elite rulers. Hence, what they do in real world to transfer greater amount of resources for themselves and to their supporters may lead to economic losses and corruption. For example, one way of such transfer to their supporters could be to allow (passively) the lower tier of political functionaries to indulge in corruption. This can be an informal tax on production and consumption, like what the mafia extracts from the traders or industrialists. This can be costlier economically because some beneficial economic activities may not take place due to the expected loss arising out of such potential payments. As some of these economic activities are based on long-term investments, a decline in such investments may lead to a dampening of economic activity for a reasonable period of time.

The counter-elites may try to extract resources from the existing capitalist (industrialist) class, as they could be seen as collaborators of the previously ruling elite. The new rulers may establish collaborative relationships with the existing industrialists over a period of time or with newer ones. Through this process, counter-elite capture may lead to a different type of crony capitalism, and in this way it may not be very different from elite capture. Counter-elites, like elites, do not have much incentive to control monopoly behaviour, since the dependence of their support base on markets could be lower, and the rulers can share a part of the extra-normal profits created. Thus, if we reckon the persistence of monopoly practice as a form of corruption, counter-elites and elites may not be significantly different when they control the government.

Another form of corruption arises out of the demand for breaking public rules created to address market failure (including public goods, externality and so on). The counter-elites, who have captured power, at the initial stages, are likely to have a lower demand for public goods in general (since their private consumption is likely to be lower). Moreover, the leaders of the counter-elites are marginally more accountable to their support base (compared to the previously ruling elites), which also have a lower demand for public goods. This may have an implication for the rule of law made for public purposes. The new rulers and their support base may not see following such rules to be very important. Moreover, the breaking of such rules through corruption could be resorted to, if it could add resources to the counter-elites for redistribution. Thus, one may see a greater tolerance of policemen collecting bribes and facilitating the breaking of rule of law or of similar acts. The difference between the elites and counter-elites here is the former's higher demand for public goods and lesser requirement to keep sections of lower tiers of rent-seekers happy.

The purpose of this section is not to argue that it is inevitable to see an increase in corruption under counter-elite capture. Instead, the position is that one should not be surprised to see an increase in corruption at this stage, even though the capture of power by the counter-elites is immensely important as part of democratisation and positive political transition.

Media and Counter-Elite Capture

Considering the importance of media in terms of governance, it is interesting to think about the place of media in counter-elite capture. In this situation, the media controlled by the state will be under the control of new rulers. Hence, this media may change itself to represent the interest of the new rulers and their constituency (within the boundary of inefficiencies inherent to such state-controlled media). On the other hand, if there were non-state media under elite capture (owned by sections of elites), it may continue to exist even under counter-elite capture if the new rulers do not ban or take over all such non-state media. This part of the media may emerge as forums for representing the interest of the previously ruling elite. This may lead to some competition within the media, provided the current rulers do not impose censorship rules.

Such censorship rules and/or a ban could happen at different stages of counter-elite capture, since they might see the existence of a media independent from the current rulers as a threat to their regime. (This is much more so when the counter-elite capture is carried out by an under-class party. We have seen the ban of all independent media in most of the socialist states, which we will discuss in the next chapter.)

However, the pre-existing independent media in certain situations, especially under social counter-elite capture, may come out with different strategies to overcome this restrictive environment. There could be strategic collaboration with the new rulers or strategic silence (including non-criticism of the government). Their interest need not be the mere existence or the profitability of the media firm. Usually media houses have interests beyond the revenue from its operation, and this could be that of furthering the interests of other businesses or at the broader level, furthering the interests of social groups working behind the media firm.

The elites even when they are out of power have some advantages, compared to non-elites when they are out of power. The former is likely to have access to financial resources, especially if the counter-elite rulers have not captured all the private assets held by the sections of elite. Even if such capturing of resources has been attempted, some of the elites may have transferred a part of the resources to outside the country or may have developed significant social capital outside, and these may help them in periods of 'oppression' by the counter-elite. Thus, they may be able to mobilise resources to sustain media representing their interest.

The presence of the media representing elite-interest and that of counter-elite through its control over state media may lead to some level of competition within media (if the system is not one of absolute dictatorship). Such competition within media may facilitate competition within politics. The competition within media and competition within politics have a correspondence relationship (one helping the other and vice versa). It is obvious that the media supporting the elite is likely to help the spread of oppositional information to a wider population in the context of counter-elite capture. Media opposing the government has an interest to enhance its subscriber base. This can gradually facilitate an adversarial public discourse within the country, and this in turn may facilitate the movement towards competitive democracy.

Evolution of the Social Counter-Elites Who Captured the State

The evolution depends partly on whether their rule is operating in a democratic context or not. In this view, one sees democracy as an exogenous variable, but the evolution of democracy can also be viewed as an endogenous process undergoing transition from elite capture to counter-elite capture and to more advanced forms of government. See Box 3.1 for a discussion on this issue.

Box 3.1:
Is Democracy Exogenous or Endogenous?

If a country is relatively uninfluenced, say through colonialism or other such processes from outside, evolution of democracy there could be mainly due to internal factors. Then one should not expect 'democracy' when it is ruled by the elites, unless the elites want to have democracy which could be less likely. The elites may prefer democracy in very rare cases, if they do not see a threat to themselves as part of democracy. A benevolent elite, who sees the need for democracy, may be needed to make it happen or such benevolence is needed even to make the population not to overthrow the elite rule under democracy. However, a counter-elite capture of the state would become relatively easier when such democracy exists.

There are not many examples of this kind from actual experience. One could see more cases where elite capture coincided with non-democratic periods. Under such a situation, counter-elite capture would take place through non-democratic means. They need not have incentives to bring in democracy immediately, especially if they are not aided by democracy-oriented outsiders. In fact, as we will discuss in the next chapter, democracy was not preferred explicitly under one form of counter-elite capture, that is, by the underclass parties. If democracy was not there as part of elite and counter-elite captures, then it could

(Box 3.1 contd)

(Box 3.1 contd)

evolve at the next stage when elites or their residuals and counter-elites compete. We will discuss this in Chapter 5.

Hence, countries which are not democratic today are predominantly sustaining either elite capture or counter-elite capture. One could see non-democratic countries in the middle east (Saudi Arabia, UAE, etc.) which are elite-capture states. Similarly, one can see non-democratic situations where counter-elites have captured the power decimating competition from previously ruling elites, and, in most cases, the captured counter-elites have become ruling elites. This is the situation in places where under-class mobilisations have captured power, such as in North Korea, Laos, Vietnam, etc. This could also be seen in a few African nations where rulers have come to power by mobilising people on the basis of ethnic or racial identity.

One could see democracy coming to exist in some countries even without an internal political transition from elite capture to counter-elite capture. The formal democracy that came to exist in India and Pakistan is an example of this case. The case of Afghanistan is another example. This was primarily due to the existence or influence of colonial rulers or other foreign governments which played an important role, at different points in history, in deciding the formal nature of the government. When one country which sustains democracy after passing through phases of elite and counter-elite capture plays an important role in deciding the nature of the government of another country, the former's notions on ideal form of government may influence the latter's transformation. Thus, we could see democracy coming to exist even in countries where elites continue to rule. Some of these countries may occasionally relapse into non-democracy, as we have seen in the case of Pakistan or Bangladesh. Thus, the existence of formal democracy in such contexts need not change the real nature of governance much, even though democracy may exert some influence on the process of transition or on the shaping of the upper boundaries of what elite or counter-elites, who capture the state, can do there. Moreover, the presence of formal democracy may change the perceptions of some people in that country on the possibilities of ordering governance.

Source: Author.

Sections of counter-elites who rule the state may gradually become elites. This could be due to different reasons. First of all, the private goods consumption of the counter-elite or the different tiers of leadership ruling the state (or those who are closer to the leaders) may improve drastically as part of state capture. Thus, they may become affluent in terms of private goods consumption. The privileged access to state power may also enhance the income or wealth status of some members of the counter-elites. Use of public resources and the resources mobilised from the capitalists, who develop a close relationship with them, could be the source of income for the leaders of counter-elites. They may not see much problem in the private use of public resources because that was more or less the practice under elite capture. There are a number of examples from India where the leaders of social counter-elite mobilisations who came from modest economic backgrounds had become economic elites after decades of leading their governments. Although they could not become dictators due to the national democracy in India, such cases could be seen in other parts of the developing world. Saddam Hussein and Gaddafi could be examples in this regard.

This ascendance to affluence which may occur among the rulers of counter-elite capture is unlikely to happen for the social group as a whole, which fought against the previously ruling elite. However, there can be different forms of legitimisation for some among the counter-elites becoming affluent and richer. They are part of the leadership, and hence higher rewards for the efforts made to mobilise people may be legitimised. There could be other identity-based rationalisations. The social group which was marginalised under the elite rule may derive certain 'happiness' in seeing that some among them could become elite with all the associated frills, and there could be attempts to rationalise the creation of such new elites.

The affluence of a section of counter-elites under their capture of the state may enhance their demand for public goods. The capitalists who develop cosy relationship with them may also pressurise them to provide more public goods. These may be in the form of infrastructure (roads, ports, other transport infrastructure, policing and so on). Thus, gradually, the counter-elites may develop incentives to provide greater amount of such public goods, even if such incentives do not exist in the beginning of the counter-elite capture. However, such improvement in the provision of public goods need not go along with an improvement in governance. This is so because the ruling counter-elites and the capitalists associated with them are likely to benefit from a filtered or mediated access to public services, in general, and also the sustenance of monopoly power.

Empirical Cases of Social Counter-Elite Capture from India and Elsewhere

Let us consider certain empirical cases of social counter-elite capture. Within India, the national elites by and large fought against British colonial rule even though there could be a few sections of elites who had collaborated with the foreign rulers. (Those sections which did not perceive to gain a grip over the post-independent governments, such as richer traders belonging to minority ethnic or social groups, could have seen collaboration with foreign rulers more beneficial than working towards independence.) Hence, the people who came to power in Indian states and at the national level after Indian independence were by and large from the national elites of different kinds (that is, economic, social, educational and so on).

Although India became democratic formally at the time of independence, it did not nullify the nature of the elite capture form of states that came to exist immediately afterwards. There was no significant opposition to the main party which led the independence struggle at the national level or in the states. The Muslim League could have become a source of anti-elite mobilisation by reckoning that the rulers belonged to the Hindu elites, but the partition of the country as part of independence had pre-empted that possibility. The main opposition to the Congress immediately after independence was from the Communist Party, but its hold was limited to a few states, and the number of seats that it could get in Parliament was much fewer compared to the ruling party. (The rightist groups, such as Jan Sangh, were also not numerically significant.)

The elites which ruled India after independence had multiple forces among them which included not only the landlords and national capitalists, but also politicians who were at the forefront of the independence struggle with different ideological leanings (and most of them came from rural or urban elite backgrounds in social and economic terms). Although the first prime minister was committed to a certain modernisation programme (which is more of a left-of-centre social democratic agenda) and he could go ahead with these ideas at the rhetorical level (and at the national or international levels to some extent), these were not translated into reality as evident from the educational or other social development indicators of the country even after the death of the first prime minster or even three to four decades after the start of independent rule. The resource allocation in many parts of India did not enable the provision of assets, such as land to the landless or education to the majority. This demonstrates the then elite capture nature of governance.

At the national level, this rule continued until the seventies. There were troubles in between. There were struggles within the elites—between leaders of the INC and the younger generation of the first prime minister. The latter could succeed that struggle with a populist agenda. In one sense, Indira Gandhi was trying to win the struggle among the elites by mobilising the poor and other sections which did not see significant gain in their life during the first two decades of independent India. However, the success of Mrs. Gandhi could not be said to have changed the character of the state substantially, but there was a greater attempt to distribute private goods (as part of what was called *Gareebi Hatao* [remove poverty] slogan), and also to 'nationalise' some private resources of the elites.

The central government of India witnessed a gradual transition towards competitive democracy from 1977, which we will discuss in Chapter 5. However, identifying a counter-elite capture at the national level in India is not that easy. The election of the first government alternative to that of the Congress in 1977 has certain characteristics of a counter-elite capture, but here the mobilisation was broad-based on pan-social groupings and was rooted in the opposition to dictatorial tendencies. The emergence of the Bharataya Janata Party (BJP) at the national level too has a few elements of counter-elite capture, as it is rooted in Hindu nationalism. The elites ruling India as part of the Congress were seen driven by a strategy of secularism, and the mobilisation of the BJP was on the slogan of neglecting majority Hindu pride or interests due to the alleged placating of the interests of the minority or as part of an elitist notion of modernity (or a neglect of traditional and nationalist interests).

However, social counter-elite capture could be seen clearly in Indian states and what we see at the national level is an aggregation of these changes in different states. Congress-led governments came to exist in Indian states immediately after independence, and these can be called elite rules or captures. The first time when an opposition party/group/coalition captured the government in each state could be an important milestone. In certain cases, this could be due to counter-elite capture, depending on the nature of political mobilisation defeating the Congress. (However, in certain other cases, the government that came to power defeating the Congress could be controlled by another section of elites, or the change in government could be due to the competition between different elite-controlled parties.) A counter-elite capture of government occurred first in the state of Kerala in 1957, but that is taken up in the next chapter in which we consider underclass captures. The next in line was in Tamil Nadu when Dravida Munnetra Kazhagam (DMK) captured power from the Congress in the late sixties.[2] Probably, this is the first social counter-elite capture in India. The mobilisation of the party was against upper caste, it was against rural elites, and it was asserting on the basis of a linguistic, regional and to some extent an ethnic (Dravidian) identity. It became active from the early fifties and rode on a number of populist agitations. Even before the capture of power,

---

[2] For a description of the political economy transition in Tamil Nadu, see MIDS (1988).

it could force the Congress-led (elite controlled) governments to yield on a number of schemes that favoured the non-elite sections of the society. Reservation in employment and education for middle and lower caste groups was one among them. At the beginning or at the initial phase of this social counter-elite capture, the leaders of DMK were not part of the economic elites in Tamil Nadu. (The split of the DMK in 1971 has also led to the competition of these splinter groups, and this has led to the emergence of competitive democracy in Tamil Nadu. We will discuss it in Chapter 5.)

Although the state of West Bengal had a non-Congress government in the seventies, it needs to be counted as a counter-elite capture; this is discussed along with the situation in Kerala as a part of under-class capture in the next chapter. The next clear example of a social counter-elite capture was in Andhra Pradesh (AP).[3] The Congress was winning all elections in the state until 1983 (from the time of its formation). The state had to wait for the emergence of the Telugu Desam party in the eighties to have such a successful counter-elite mobilisation. The major mobilisation was on the basis of Telugu pride against the national leaders of the Congress, which changed the state chief ministers very frequently. There was also a flavour of middle-caste mobilisation against the ruling elites (Congress) controlled by upper castes (Reddies). The fact that the leader of this counter-elite mobilisation was a part of the regional economic elite does not change the basic character of the counter-elite nature of this political mobilisation.

Maharashtra started witnessing the emergence of a social mobilisation in the eighties in the form of Shiva Sena. Although the state had a longer history of lower-caste mobilisation, it was not successful in capturing the state. The Shiva Sena is rooted in regional pride and identity. The perception that the local people are not benefitting from the economic opportunities and resources of the Bombay metropolitan area was used for such mobilisation. It has been argued that the lower-middle class from the state who

---

[3] The description of this political transition and its impact on welfare programmes can be seen in Mukund (1990) and Suri (2003).

did not get enough employment opportunities in Bombay became the major support base of the Shiva Sena (Katzenstein, 1979). Hence, the assertion of the Shiva Sena could be termed as part of a social counter-elite mobilisation. The emergence of the BJP in a number of states could be due to a set of factors, and all of them could not be termed as social counter-elite capture. Its constituent part, Jan Sangh or its social organisation, namely the Rashtriya Swayamsevak Sangh (RSS), existed even during the freedom struggle, and this could indicate that these were alternatives to the Congress as focal point of political mobilisation during the freedom struggle. One could see a Hindu Jan Sangh, Muslim League and centrist Congress as three political formations during colonial India, probably all controlled by the elites from respective sections of the society and with different ideological or cultural viewpoints.

The Jan Sangh or its larger form BJP could become the rallying point of oppositional politics in a number of Indian states when people became disappointed with the ruling Congress party for different reasons. Hence, the emergence of the BJP in states like Madhya Pradesh, Gujarat, Himachal Pradesh or even Uttar Pradesh (UP) and Chhattisgarh need not be seen as outcomes of social counter-elite captures. There could be cases where the BJP might have used social identities strategically by having middle-caste state leaders (for example, Uma Bharathi or Kalyan Singh) to mobilise support against the Congress in these states. However, these strategies did not sustain longer as the support base of the BJP was strongly grounded among the social and economic elites of the country (including its trading class). There were situations where the BJP mobilised the Hindu majority as against what they called the pseudo-secularism of the Congress. Hence, the ascendance of the BJP in a number of states cannot be termed clearly as social counter-elite capture based on the framework used here.

The clearer cases of social counter-elite captures have occurred in India in the nineties in UP and Bihar. The emergence of political parties led by Mulayam Singh Yadav in UP and Lalu Prasad Yadav in Bihar are cases of middle-caste mobilisations leading to counter-elite captures of the state. In both these states, these middle-caste leaders have not only used their own social groups (which were perceiving marginalisation by the upper castes), but have also developed close coalitions with the minority community (Muslims) which was also perceiving marginalisation by the majority community.[4] To some extent, the BJP could not sustain their mobilisations within these states even with a middle-caste leader (Kalyan Singh in UP). In addition to this, the fact that both Mulayam and Lalu have developed their movements against the BJP, which indicate that the latter's role in UP or Bihar could not be termed as social counter-elite mobilisation.

The emergence of the Bahujan Samaj Party (BSP) in UP could also be termed as a social counter-elite capture, and this lower-caste mobilisation is not only against the upper-caste elites, but also against middle-caste groups which have become rulers under the Samajwadi Party (SP). This is an interesting example of a social counter-elite mobilisation against a formation which itself was part of a counter-elite mobilisation. The emergence of Nitish Kumar is not viewed in this regard, and it could be seen as part of a competition within middle-caste counter-elite mobilisation which started under the leadership of Lalu Prasad Yadav. (This competition within a counter-elite mobilisation is an interesting issue in competitive populism or democracy and will be discussed in Chapter 5.) Although the political base of Ram Vilas Paswan in Bihar could be termed as lower-caste mobilisation, it was not successful in capturing the government there. Jharkhand Mukti Morcha could be yet another social counter-elite mobilisation based on ethnic-regional basis, but their success in capturing the state on its own is also limited. There have been regional assertions in many parts of India including the Northern hills in the state of West Bengal, Telangana in AP, etc. Although the National Conference in Kashmir had been competing and collaborating with the Congress, it could be called an assertion led by the local elite against the national elite.

---

[4] Mulayam Singh and Lalu Prasad, though they are influenced by a socialist ideology, their practical politics centred on mobilising specific caste and community groups.

Social Counter-Elite Captures in Other Parts of the World

There are a number of social counter-elite captures in other parts of the world. Almost all freedom struggles had the feature of a social counter-elite assertion (since the struggles were based on national identity), but many of the post-independent governments in the colonies were in the hands of, or captured by, the domestic elites. One of the earliest social counter-elite assertions was in Haiti, where the Blacks brought in as workers overthrew the French colonial rulers. A classic case in this regard in the twentieth century is the anti-Apartheid Movement and the emergence of the black-dominated government in South Africa. The fact that the previous rulers were representing minority, descendants of the past colonialists and were also racially different from the ruled, and the perceived and actual exclusion of the ruled in different spaces by the government have fuelled the counter-elite capture there. The majority of the ruled was also economically poor or vulnerable and this had given the anti-Apartheid Movement the form of an under-class mobilisation, but it was essentially driven by the social identity of the marginalised. Malaysia went through a period where a group (local people or Malays) asserted their rights and captured the government based on a perception of the domination of others in economic and administrative spheres. Iran had witnessed multiple social counter-elite captures. The assertion against the dictatorial government by the movement led by Islamic clerics was driven by the feeling that the ruler was not sufficiently representing the aspirations and identity of the people. Nationhood and religious identity played an important role there. Over a period of time, a perception was gathered that the elected rulers who came to power after throwing out the dictator were from liberal elites. This has led to popular assertions by those who claim to represent people at large, and also the religious values (in letter and spirit). The government led by Ahmadinejad was the outcome of such an assertion. The countries with multiple ethnic compositions could see political struggles (and attempt to capture the governments) on the basis of one or the other ethnic identity against the other. The struggle between the Indian population and the others in Fiji is one such example. The emergence of Saddam Hussein in Iraq and Gaddafi in Libya were also the products of counter-elite assertions, as the political formations or assertions which brought them to power used religious and socialist aspirations. Of course, these rulers have become parts of elites later on. The struggle within Iraq where the Kurds and Shia population wanted to assert their rights over Sunni rulers was also an example of social counter-elite assertion, although their partial success occurred only after recent foreign interventions.

There are also a number of regional or ethnic assertions within the countries, which could have led to social-counter elite assertions. When such regional or ethnic group forms the minority, the attempt would be to form a smaller state carved out from the nation ruled by the 'other' majority group. The success of this usually needs the help of external forces or some window of opportunities. The former Yugoslavia got fragmented along social or ethnic identities after the disappearance of the dictatorial socialist state. The formation of the smaller nations within the former Soviet Union was along social, ethnic or regional lines, even though some of these new nations were captured by the local elites. Examples like East Timor reflect the role of the international community. There were also a number of assertions by the social counter-elites who failed or are not successful in capturing or creating their own state. The Tibetans in China and the Tamils in Sri Lanka are some of the well-known examples.

In certain other cases, counter-elite assertions need not capture the state, but the ruling elites may yield to the demands for reforming the state/governance/allocation of public resources. This is also an important part of the democratisation process. Such adjustments include the creation of autonomous governance mechanisms for the asserting counter-elites or granting special privileges, packages and resource allocation programmes for the people who took part in these struggles. This may lead to a greater allocation of resources for the private goods consumption of the people who were struggling. It may also lead to greater consumption of private goods, including education, by them. It may reduce the public resources for the state ruled by the other group (or that social group which control the state). The central government of India has accommodated a number of such regional aspirations within its nationhood or within the states. The autonomous council in Darjeeling and that in the state of Tripura for the tribal population are examples. The formation of states in India on the basis of language itself was based on the recognition of the aspirations of specific social groups. Foreigners settled in countries like United States, Canada, Australia, and New Zealand have designed specific resource allocation programmes for the indigenous people, and these are also part of the accommodation of the interests of diverse social groups. The potential threats from assertions based on social identity have encouraged many countries to make these adjustments within the nationhood.

What Is Wrong with the Social Counter-Elite Capture?

Counter-elite capture is an important, and, to some extent, an unavoidable part of democratisation, as a step forward from elite capture. However, any ruling party (or for that matter, any provider or supplier of goods and services) wants to have monopoly. Even those governments which are committed to democracy would like to be re-elected with minimal opposition. The counter-elites who capture power, sometimes through democratic routes, want to retain power for ever. Depending on the nature of the opposition within the society, counter-elites who capture power may turn out to be the political elites. Then all the undesirable features of elite capture that we discussed in the previous chapter would become relevant also for the counter-elite capture. These are not repeated here.

The absence of adequate political competition, whether it is under-elite or counter-elite capture, has two implications. There are not enough incentives for the government to perform. There is not even adequate pressure to distribute private goods among all sections of population. This can happen even under social counter-elite capture. This is so because the counter-elite is from one social group, and there could be other non-elite groups for whom the ruling counter-elite may not feel a need to distribute private goods. Hence even for the expansion of private goods, political competition is necessary, and thus a polity trapped in counter-elite capture could be harmful.

Some Ideological Issues as Part of Social Counter-Elite Capture

The fact that the counter-elites capturing state come from one social group defined in terms of an identity has implications for the ideological contours of the social change. This is so because one identity is preserved usually in opposition to other identities. Thus, the religion underlying the counter-elite capture may create an adversarial situation for other religions. Each religion may have ideas of social organisations (different to counter ideas in other religions), and these too may play a role under counter-elite capture. This may not be equally true for caste, ethnic, regional or race based identities. However, each identity is likely to have some special features, and these could be partly generated as part of their social and economic development. There would be some pressure to maintain these identifying features, as social identity plays an important role in legitimising the counter-elite capture that we have discussed in this chapter. The need to focus on one set of features defining an identity would mean some intentional or unintentional efforts to undermine the features of other identities. Some of these identities need not change as part of socio-economic development, unlike class. Hence, ideological discourses and social organisations in such a society could be static and fragmentary, or the process of social change itself could move along highly contested territories.

There is one more impact. A focus on the specific features of social identity would also mean certain reluctance to move ahead in terms of modernisation. A social group has certain discerning features (including their norms), and these could be the product of their current status in terms of socio-economic evolution. However, an identity-based politics (and an effort to capture power) or the need to legitimise political actions on the basis of social identity would mean certain compulsion to grant some ultimate truth or relevance status to the specific features of this identity by neglecting the fact that these features may change as part of the socio-economic evolution. This would create an unwillingness to move ahead, and hence they may encourage people to work against such evolution which may change these defining features. This can be a major threat to the transition towards modernity. This can be seen very clearly in those counter-elite captures driven by religious identities. Even those mobilisations which are formed against caste discrimination could not get out of the compulsions of the fragmentary caste system. Hence, the middle-caste assertions against upper caste could fail to incorporate lower castes within their fold.

Threats to Social Counter-Elites Who Capture the State

There are two major generic sources of threat to the social counter-elites who capture the state. First is from the elites who were ruling previously. In many situations, even after the counter-elite capture, certain elements of previously ruling elite would be 'live' or active within the society. This is especially so when these elites have the support of some social groups (identity), and when they are not some 'rootless' dictators or external rulers. The people who are unhappy with the counter-elite who rule the state may gravitate towards sections of previously ruled group when they are active. This is more likely to happen if there are no other politically mobilised groups with sufficient hold in such a society.

There are obvious and not so obvious reasons for the previously ruling elites to be unhappy under counter-elite rule. The private transfers enjoyed by them would decline under the new rule. Moreover, there could be a decline in the public goods based on the yardstick of the previously ruling (relatively wealthier) elites because of the need for diverting a major part of the public resources for the enhanced coverage of private goods distribution under counter-elite rule. Hence, not only the elites, but the wealthier or affluent sections in general could become unhappy under the counter-elite capture. The fact that a section of the ruling counter-elites could gradually become economically well off as part of their rule may partly reduce their legitimacy as an anti-elite force. This too may encourage the reassertion of the previously ruling elites. However, when they reassert, they realise that they cannot recapture the state merely based on their strength. They need greater support or higher level of legitimisation to recapture from the counter-elites who have captured the state. Hence, they would be more responsive to the needs of the non-elites and be a little more sensitive to their own use of public resources for private goods consumption, if they were interested in recapturing the power.

The second source of threat to social counter-elites who capture the state may come from other social groups which feel marginalised under the ruling counter-elites. For example, in states where middle castes have captured power (from the previously ruling upper-caste elites) there could be lower-caste mobilisation which might threaten the middle-caste rulers. The conflict between SP and BSP in UP is an important example in this regard. Similarly, when people from one religion or an ethnic group or a region forms the counter-elite rulers, there could be other ethnic, religious or regional groups which might emerge as counter-elites working against the currently ruling counter-elites. If N.T. Rama Rao could use Andhra pride as a mobilisation strategy in the state of AP, the Telangana Movement is asserting as a sub-regional identity within the state.

There could also be a coalition of the elites and those sections of non-elites who are unhappy with the ruling counter-elites. Such coalitions would also 'democratise' the concerns of the elites. They would be forced to bring in the needs of the non-elites into their political agenda. Hence, even if elites recapture power after counter-elite capture, the way the government functions would be significantly different from that under elite capture. The threats encountered by the ruling counter-elites may lead to the evolution of the polity into a competitive democracy eventually, if not immediately. We will consider this in the chapter on competitive populism (Chapter 5). But before that we need to consider the other kind of counter-elite capture, that is, the capture of the state by the under-class party.

4

Under-Class Capture of the State

When the majority of society (including the poorer or under-privileged ones) other than the elites feel excluded or marginalised by the elite-captured state, one response could be the resistance based on their economic status. Here, people belonging to somewhat similar economic conditions revolt against the state and capture it. This is not at all a hypothetical situation as evident from the history. The socialist revolutions that took place in many parts of the world in the twentieth century were an outcome of this class-based uprising. Even without such revolutions, there could be political formations of underclass capturing power through democratic processes. The rise of labour or socialist parties in West European countries is an example. The formation of the first government in the state of Kerala in India by the Communist Party of India was also one such case.

All the people who are part of such class-based action need not come from the working class or the poorer sections of the society. There could be a leadership emerging from the affluent or middle class channelising the anger of, and giving an ideological character to, this class-based resistance. The leadership of the communist parties in the Soviet Union or other countries, including China, came from these backgrounds. In these cases, the discontent with the elites, including feudal landlords and other wealthier sections, that existed among different sections of society was channelised to create a movement capable to capture the state through non-democratic (through violent or non-violent) means. A lot has been written on socialist states or governments controlled by the communist parties, and this chapter does not intent to repeat them.

What is attempted here is to outline the features of governance in such states based on the framework used in this book.

The features of governance under dictatorial socialist states (one form of under-class capture) and in those nations where under-class parties govern within a framework of democracy are different (even though there are some similarities.) We will consider them separately.

Impact of Under-Class Capture Leading to Socialist States

Under-class capture in socialist states had led to the near destruction of certain power structures that existed in those societies, and were affecting the daily life of the people. For example, it could change the feudal land relations which existed in rural areas. This could be due to the change in land ownership from landlords or kinship systems to the government, as occurred in most of the socialist states. This could have reduced the dependence of the agricultural tenants (cultivating farmers) on the land-owning class. A similar structural change could take place with respect to the capitalist–labour relations. In full-fledged socialist states, the ownership of capital moved from specific industrialists to the state. However, capitalism was not well developed in those countries which moved to socialism in the early part of the twentieth century. These changes in asset ownership and the near destruction of the existing power structures would empower substantial sections of people belonging to the under-class. It is not implied here that all sections of the economic under-class would feel the same level of empowerment, or that there would not be any social group (belonging to economic under class) which feels left out of this process of empowerment.

The creation of socialist states in such countries had also destroyed certain other social barriers that existed between ethnic groups or other social classes. For example, there could be a state-led integration in imparting the same language through education and/or not recognising the cultural specificities of specific minority groups. Such integration could take violent or coercive forms, and one could see ethnic or social groups resisting such integration. The case of Tibetans in China is well known. However, the impact of this integration is that mainland China is much less divided according to ethnicity or social identity today (say, compared to contemporary India). However, we could see a return of the dominance of social identities in social and political life as the centralised socialist state fell apart as in the Soviet Union. Many Central Asian republics (which were part of the former Soviet Union) legitimise their independence (and autocratic regimes) on the basis of ethnic and religious grounds.

To some extent, the capture of power by the parties representing the economic under-class, especially in socialist countries, had also resulted in certain changes in the power structure within the households. Provision of education to all including girls and of employment opportunities to women had created a situation where women took active participation in the economic life in many socialist countries. (Such participation need not have led to an equally important role for women in political life.) Thus, their dependence on men/husbands/families for social and financial security had declined. This also changed the bargaining power between men and women regarding marital, sexual and reproductive relations. One could see some reversal in this regard too in some regions, such as Central Asia, when they came out of socialism.

Under-Class Capture and the Provision of Private Goods

The overthrow of the elite rule by the under-class party would lead to a wider distribution of private goods by the state. In fact, the capture of state by the under-class could lead to a much wider distribution of private goods (or transfer) cutting across the boundaries of social groups (compared to that by social counter-elites).

A wider set of private goods, including food, other basic goods, primary education and health care, housing, electricity, were provided by these states to almost all individuals without considering their affordability. Alternatively, it was considered that taking care of the (basic) private goods consumption was the responsibility of the state. Since these goods are distributed widely without using markets, there is a need for rationing, and hence people may not receive the quantity or quality that they like to have.

This wider distribution of private goods has created important benefits. In terms of literacy, basic education and primary health care, almost all the socialist countries were much ahead of the other parts of the developing world. This has improved clearly the education and health dimensions of the human development indicators, although the impact on economic growth was not so clear. The other type of counter-elite capture too had resulted in the widening of distribution of private goods; the socialist states were remarkable in terms of their positive impacts on education and health outcomes.

It could be possible that some sections of social groups who might not have collaborated with the under-class party could have felt excluded under such a regime. For example, ethnic groups, such as the Tibetans or those living in western China and similar other localities who were unwilling to integrate well with the nation-building project of the Chinese Communist party were excluded by the communist-led state there. However, even in those cases the real issue was not an under-provision of private goods by the state. For example, there were attempts to provide primary education in all parts of China, but the Tibetans might have felt uneasy about the uniform nature of this education provided.

Such a wider coverage of private goods becomes possible in socialist states due to the ownership of almost all the resources by the state. (There were inefficiencies in the production or distribution of private goods due to the central planning system, and these will be discussed later in the chapter.) The rulers here tried to bring in the private assets held by all, including the previously ruling elites under state ownership (that is, through nationalisation).

Provision of Public Goods

The impact on public goods and services was somewhat different in various socialist countries. All these countries tried hard to provide safe drinking water, public health facilities and those related to the basic survival of their population. If we analyse the Soviet Union or East European socialist countries, there were enough efforts to provide public goods and infrastructure required for a modern economy by the state. East European territories had a shared history of development with other parts of Europe, these were in a 'modernisation competition' with West Europe or the United States (US), starting with the Second World War, and the features, such as public ownership of almost all resources of the country, relatively small population density, and so on could have helped this set of socialist countries to provide public goods and services to its people somewhat matching with those available in the developed western world.

Probably, the supply of public goods was relatively easier under the central planning model. This was so because the government could easily plan and implement public goods projects wanted by it, without being hampered by the needs to encounter the democratic pulls of different sections of the society. They could take over private land-holdings for public purposes, create new cities, and transfer population settlements, and carry out such large-scale social interventions without bothering much about the actual or potential social unrests in this regard. The prestige attached to the creation of modern infrastructure, the ability to use labour within the economy without paying its opportunity cost, the ability to mobilise domestic savings somewhat coercively without paying its market returns, the perceived or real needs of national defence, all have facilitated the creation of infrastructure (roads, airports, ports, railways, science laboratories and so on) in these countries.

However, countries, such as China, though excelled in the provision of basic health care and primary education could not provide much modern infrastructure until its change in economic policy framework in the late seventies, which resulted in the greater focus on export of its products to the global markets and more inflow of investments from elsewhere (and higher levels of economic growth). However, the fact that modern infrastructure could not be built adequately in some of the socialist countries, such as China, (before the seventies) need not be seen negatively, as the demand for such public goods would have also been lower there considering the lower levels of per-capita income or consumption of their citizens. Thus, the provision of public goods was by and large in tandem with the consumption needs of these societies at their early stages.

Impact of Ideology on Economic Development

In general, the socialist parties have a particular ideology of economic development. This ideology motivates people to work for social change beyond the limitations of status quo, and it is important in deciding the nature of governance. In general, ideology can also become a marker of social identity, or those who believe in a particular ideology may constitute a social identity later on. Or it is also possible that some of the social identities, especially that of religions, such as Christianity, Islam or sub-groups (Catholics or Protestants), may have come to exist due to a particular ideology or a vision of a desired private or social life.

There is no surprise that the social movement of people who are economically under-privileged develop (or is centred around) an economic ideology. There is no surprise again that the main objective of such an ideology is to counter the then prevailing economic practices, and to come out with an alternative vision of organising economy and society. Because of these organic reasons, and also due to historical and/or incidental reasons, Marxism or different versions of it guided the movements of the under-class almost all over the world during the last century. It perceived a greater role for the state in driving matters related to the economy, as markets were seen to be reproducing inequalities in conventional economies.

It is well known that this ideology had an impact on the path of economic development of the states captured by the economic under-class. The way it has unfolded, its impact and the final transition are discussed widely in the literature. Only a few points are mentioned here. In societies where under-class parties could establish non-democratic regimes, almost all the assets have come under public ownership. Production and distribution of goods and services were driven by the central planning process. Market was not allowed to function not only in commodity markets, but also in labour and capital markets. The capital investments and technological change in the economy were also driven by the state. In such situations, the state replaced almost all the capitalists.

This model did lead to economic development in some contexts. However, these were based on the intensive use of capital (as in the Soviet Union) or labour (as in China). Technology and education in the socialist world did not contribute as much to the productivity growth of the economy as in non-socialist developed economies (Hayami & Godo, 1997). Or the processes in the economy were not conducive enough to translate those developments in science, technology and higher education into productivity improvements in the economy. Hence, there were limitations in producing goods and services demanded by the people, and they faced severe shortages. The demand and supply for the inputs in the production system could not be matched well by the allocation processes of the central planning system. Since the distribution of almost all categories of private goods was taken over theoretically by the state (by replacing market), the inefficiencies in the process have led to a situation where people do not get adequate quantity of such goods.

Although the ideology driving the organisation of the economy had similarity between different socialist countries, the economic outcomes were different in different countries based on other factors. This is to be expected because the socialist system created closed economies, and hence the outcomes and the transition path of these economies would be determined by internal factors. The population density, availability of labour and other natural resources, size of the country and so on could have played an important role. Thus, socialist Russia could develop to the level of a middle-income European economy, whereas the achievements in terms of income in countries, such as China/Cuba/Laos/North Korea, with different internal factors were different. Hence, China in the pre-seventies was a relatively poorer agricultural economy with certain levels of social development (in terms of primary education and healthcare) and countries, such as Cuba or Laos, were depending on the aid or favourable terms of trade with the socialist block for most of their income. Thus, the closeness of the economy, although it has not affected the modernisation of the production much in Russia or east European countries, it affected the transition of countries, such as China or Vietnam, or it has enhanced the dependence of countries such as Cuba, North Korea or Laos, until their transition to the market economies. The latter set of countries faced a very difficult situation when the socialist block collapsed in the early nineties.

Whatever be the appropriateness of the above description of the efficacy of central planning, one thing is clear that none of these socialist countries could sustain their centrally planned economic systems. Some of them (for example, the Soviet Union) have overthrown their political and economic systems, whereas countries, such as China and Vietnam, have attempted to use market economy within the one-party political system. The remaining socialist countries, such as Cuba or North Korea, are either struggling to change or grappling with an unacceptable quality of life for the majority of their citizens. Although the growth pattern of the western developed nations and their international efforts to curb the spread of communism too have played a role in initiating changes in the socialist countries, the role of internal economic problems and the demand for change cannot be underestimated.

Hence, despite substantial improvements in human development and important strides made in science, technology and higher education, and also a reasonable provision of public goods, socialist countries could not pursue their selected path of economic growth on a sustainable basis. The difficulties encountered by their people in meeting their private goods demands, perceived need for enhancing personal income or wealth along with the growing demand for individual freedom and political rights have ignited their transition towards market economies.

Impact of Under-Class Party on Governance

The socialist states had their own notions of good governance, and it is obvious that such notions are different from those prevalent in modern liberal democracies. For example, take the case of the separation of powers between the legislature, executive and judiciary, which is a corner stone of governance in liberal democracy. This is not respected well within the socialist single-party rules, where even the judiciary is not seen really as to be independent. (In reality, the liberal democratic notions of governance are not taken seriously even under elite or social counter-elite captures, but there is no major theoretical opposition to such notions under these rules.) Thus, there were only limited expectations on the part of the people that they could use judiciary to get justice against the excesses, if any, of the executive and the ruling party.

There was not enough separation between the business enterprises and government. Even if market economy was used, government had full or part ownership of many business enterprises providing private goods. Thus, the interests of the owner of these enterprises and the interests of the society as a whole got mixed, and it could create problems under certain situations. Some business enterprises tried to acquire monopoly power based on their closeness to the government. Governments were not that interested in establishing competition even when it was beneficial to the consumers.

The meddling of the state in the management of business enterprises in such situations prevented the realisation of the true value of different inputs, including the savings of the people. There were artificially low interest rates in the economy when governments tried to meddle with capital markets to make the cost of capital lower. Governments played an excessive role in determining wages and salaries in firms. Even when such countries sustain markets, government intervention would affect land markets wherein people would be forced to surrender their lands and other assets without getting their actual opportunity costs. For example, regulations regarding the acquisition of land could be vague and could provide little protection to those who use land in such situations.

The continued part-ownership of the business enterprises by the state, and also the meddling by the state in the management of such firms, could prevent the emergence of a professional capitalist class in the society which could survive in a competitive economy. There could also be a mixing of the regulatory and executive powers of the state. Controlling monopoly, which we have mentioned in the previous paragraph, is one such regulatory role. In order to see that environment is not harmed or safety is not compromised through the actions of the arms of the government, such separation of regulatory powers from the management of enterprise would be required.[1] The absence of such separation has also led to an inadequate enforcement of environment and safety regulations.

It is not that the socialist parties were unconcerned about the need to have mechanisms to discipline individuals in the government, including its own party members and leaders, on one hand; however, they visualised such disciplining through the internal democracy of the party. On the other hand, one could see a number of limitations for this party democracy. The party, as a subset of the society, need not always represent the interests of the wider society, and the absence of a society-wide democracy was found to be costly later. The hierarchical structure within the party and the aspirations of its ordinary members to go up in the hierarchy would also mean that the leaders could control and manipulate party democracy to serve their interests or strengthen their views. We have seen cases where individual leaders acquiring a very dominant position within these parties and their excesses could be corrected only after their death or incapacitation.

---

[1] Separation of powers is needed to avoid the conflict of interest, and to see that each arm or agency takes actions which it is supposed to take (and do not take those which it is not supposed to take).

Corruption under One-Party Rule of the Under-Class

There is not much use in discussing the corruption under conventional socialism these days, because almost all such countries which sustained these central planning systems have moved towards a market economy. Hence, what is important is to understand the nature of corruption in countries, such as China, Vietnam, Laos, (and possibly Cuba) which have opened up their economies, but the governance is kept under the control of communist or socialist party.

At one level, these parties share some commonalities with the social counter-elite political formations. Both represent (or draw strength from claiming to represent) non-elites. The fact that they were successful in countering elites and in coming to power shows their support base among the sections which were not comfortable with the elite rule. This is what has encouraged them to redistribute a greater part of the public resources to the non-elite support base. However, this may encourage the new rulers to rewrite the rules on public resources, and thus bringing more of them under their control. Or the notion of what is public or private can change under these dispensations. This by itself need not be reckoned as corruption—even though this can be costly in economic terms. It may create uncertainty in the minds of economic investors or actors because they may become uncertain of the nature of the property rights—whether something is private or public may become uncertain. Some of the private assets may become legally public under such one-party rule, and this cannot be called (legal) corruption even though it can lead to (economic) inefficiencies. The way such assets are managed by the public authorities may not be conducive to maximise the social gains from them.

There are some obvious differences between under-class parties and social counter-elite political formations in this regard. First of all, there is a systematic organisation that connects and leads the under-class parties. In certain cases as in North Korea, the leader and the organisation may become synonymous, and in that case one may not see much difference in this regard. But in many other communist or socialist parties, the organisational structure was intact and they had some influence on the leaders. Secondly, the under-class parties are driven by some ideological legitimacy.[2] The organisational rules and ideology together may moderate corruption in under-class parties to some extent. These may encourage such parties to take some actions against corrupt individuals. This is seen in China today.

Another factor that moderates the need for corruption in one-party rule is the lack of democracy itself. Democracy may put some pressure to create and extent support base, and this could lead to what can be called ad-hoc redistribution. This redistribution may manifest in two forms (as we have discussed in the previous chapter): (a) The government extracting resources from the economy and distributing it among the current or would be supporters; (b) Allowing supporters to 'tax' their local economy—it could be 'rent-seeking' from those around. In poorer countries, the opportunity to carry out (a) is limited, and hence (b) is tolerated, if not encouraged, by governments which want to extend their support base. The latter way of redistribution can increase corruption. Since the socialist states do not entertain democracy, there is not much pressure on the governments to allow such decentralised 'taxation'.

When communist or socialist dictators followed socialism/central planning/state ownership as the guiding principle of organising economy, it had a dampening impact on mutually beneficial transactions. This could hamper their economic growth. However, this is not a serious problem when such governments encourage markets and private investments. It is not unusual to see such governments or their political functionaries or their agents charging (or taxing) the economic transactions formally and informally. In that sense, it could be similar to any other counter-elite political formation. However, the aforementioned factors may be moderating the impulses of personal corruption in under-class party rules.

Thus, the central argument of this section is that even when under-class party rules are similar to social counter-elite capture,

---

[2] Some of the social counter-elite political formations could also be drawing strength from ideological positions (of say, against upper caste/dominant race/ethnic groups/foreigners/for nationalism).

one should not be surprised to see lesser corruption under the governments ruled by such parties in a legal sense (compared to other non-elite formations). One important factor that encourages corruption (and illegal behaviour) under elite and counter-elite capture including that by an under-class party is the absence of a free media. It takes time to develop competitive media in societies where under-class parties have established dictatorial governments. This is so because they would try to decimate the elites by capturing their assets. This prevents the sustenance of any media funded by non-ruling elites in such societies. Moreover, under-class parties may use their internal mechanisms (party, secret agents and police) to prevent the circulation of counter-information within the society. This could be through the suppression of all actors who seem to be disseminating all such information. Of course, there could be information circulation driven by external forces in such contexts. The anti-communist campaign driven by the liberal developed countries in the erstwhile socialist countries is one such example. However, the limited circulation of the anti-state information by the domestic actors in under-class party states could be a factor facilitating corruption and other illegalities.

Under-Class Party Rules in Democracies

Under-class parties get elected to form government in different ways. This may happen in a situation where democracy exists formally and/or through competition between different sections of the elites (or between elites and sections of non-elites). In such a context, a political formation based on economic class can emerge among the poorer and working-class people, and it can win elections. This happens through the process of deepening democracy. For example, in the context where formal democracy manifests itself in competition between different sections of elites, the non-elite sections which were initially behaving as vote banks (or were excluded from electoral process as the voting rights are limited to only certain sections of society, such as the landed male) would become politically active gradually, and left-of-centre political formations may emerge to capture their aspirations. Or one of the competing parties may reinvent itself to represent the interests of the under-class in such societies. These have happened in the democracies of the Western Europe or North America. If we analyse the history of the Labour Party in Britain, the Socialist Party in France and the Social Democratic Party in Germany, we can see their origins (for example, in trade union movements) or transformations to represent the non-elite sections and their attempts to capture the governments. All these parties came to power in the early decades of the twentieth century (around the same time, socialist parties were capturing state and converting these into totalitarian ones in parts of East Europe and Asia). The Democratic Party of the US too had counted the support of the small farmers and urban working class. There are two impacts due to the political assertion of the non-elites: the mobilisation of such non-elite groups may encourage the elite-controlled states to distribute more public resources to a wider section of the society. The attempt by the government of Bismarck in Germany to have a mandatory health insurance or policy could be reckoned as one such example. The control of the governments later by the left-of-centre or socialist parties have led to much more drastic improvements in resource transfer to the poor and working class, and to the evolution of comprehensive social security schemes.

There are also a few situations where under-class parties mobilised people against the elites who controlled the governments even at an early stage of democratisation. The case of communist-controlled state governments in India is of this kind. These developing societies where communist parties got elected to rule, such as in Kerala or West Bengal, through democracy faced different kind of challenges. These parties were unable to convert the states into totalitarian ones because these state governments operated within a national constitution which ensured the existence of formal democracy (and these parties did not have the majority support at the national level to change the constitution). There were other developing countries as well (such as Costa Rica or Nicaragua in

Central America) where left-of-centre or socialist parties which came to power, but could not (or did not) establish totalitarian states for different reasons. Sri Lanka also had a long history of political mobilisation of the workers and under-class based on different shades of socialist leanings,[3] and this had also influenced the policies of post-independent governments there.

However, these countries continued to be open economies, and the ascendance of socialist parties to power could not change this basic character. Similarly, they could not nationalise all private firms or abolish private property, as these governments were in a democratic framework and there were opposition from different quarters—elites or land-owning class, an independent judiciary or media. These states could not increase taxes in any unusual manner for the same reasons.

However, such under-class parties have encountered greater pressure and showed interest to distribute public resources for the private goods of the majority. Hence, even in democratic regimes, under-class parties used a greater part of the public resources for the distribution of private goods to wider sections of society. There could be greater efforts to provide food, primary education, housing, primary health care, etc. to the needy by the governments of these under-class parties. However, the resource base that these governments have or autonomy of the state in terms of mobilising resources is rather limited compared to that of a socialist state.

The communist or socialist parties which come to power through democracies have also attempted certain structural changes (although they cannot match the socialist states in this regard). Land reforms—giving ownership rights to tenants, taking over 'surplus' land from those who have more land, redistribution of land to the landless—were attempted with different degrees of success. For example, the Communist Party which came to power in a democratic context tried to implement land reforms in case of West Bengal and Kerala, although not on a comprehensive basis.

---

[3] Some of these movements, such as the Janathā Vimukthi Peramuna (JVP), became more nationalistic or ethnocentric later.

The governments controlled by the under-class parties in democracies could exercise only an indirect pressure on the capitalists. One such way was through militant labour struggles in the industrial enterprises for a higher share of the surplus as wages and indirect support of the government for such labour actions. Hence, the capitalists may not get adequate protection from these states for their (private) property (and probably for their life), if these are at stake as part of their conflict with the labour.

In situations of elite capture or social counter-elite capture, there are avenues for capitalists to collaborate with the state through mutually beneficial transactions. This could take the form of buying politicians by the capitalists in certain cases. It is through such collaboration that capitalists get the protection of the state and also the service of the state in solving coordination problems in the management of firms (including the taming of aggressive labour) in societies where 'law and order' is yet to be developed on the lines of liberal democracies. However, such collaboration with capitalists becomes very difficult for a communist or socialist party for ideological reasons. (It may be noted that such collaboration has developed reasonably well when socialist states moved towards market economy.) Even if collaborative relationship develops between specific leaders of the party and capitalists, these can be questioned from within the party or can delegitimise the party. This may prevent the rulers from providing reliable signals to the potential investors. This too could discourage capitalists from investing in states controlled by under-class parties. However, the open economy nature of these states ensured that the former could move the capital out of these territories. Thus, there could be a flight of capital and investments from such societies controlled by the communist or socialist parties (unless they reinvent themselves as social democratic parties with friendly relationship with capitalists). This could have a negative impact on their domestic economic growth.

Whatever be the nature of relationship between the underclass party and capitalists, such a party has to allow the functioning of private enterprises by choice or compulsions (if these are not centrally planned states where all production is taken over by the government). By and large, the party may want to have a closer relationship with (or a control over) these enterprises. It can lead to two problems: too much control may lead to lack of enough space for private investors, and this may dampen investments. This control would also mean greater extraction of resources by the state (or by the labour through state patronage) more often through non-transparent (such as non-tax) means. The other problem, usually arising out of the outcome of the first one, is a too cosy relationship of the party with specific capitalists or enterprises. This may lead to monopoly in commodity or service markets for some enterprises or monopsony in input markets. The state may also try to intervene in the input markets on behalf of the enterprises. This may manifest in much more coercive acquisition of land and ad-hoc allocation of natural resources. This can happen even when the enterprises are fully owned by the government.

The slow pace of economic development driven by dampened private investments and the concern of these ruling parties to expand private goods to most of the under-privileged sections together have some implications. A greater part of the public resources (and, here, there are limits to the increase in tax rates) have to be used for such private goods distribution. This would mean that adequate public goods cannot be supplied even when these are needed for the growth of the economy. When tax resources are inadequate, the states may borrow (if possible) to expand the distribution of private goods and limited public goods. There could be an increase in the debt burden or an erosion of the repayment capability of the state. This could lead to macro-economic imbalances, reduction in credit worthiness, devaluation of the currency and so on. This would again become another dis-incentive for the capitalists to sustain industrial production there. The low level of investments may lead to supply bottlenecks for the goods and services, and these can fuel inflation.

However, the open-economy nature of the society would create a situation where a section of those people affected by the low economic development would migrate. (Although there were migrations from socialist countries, it was through a difficult process due to the internal restrictions there.) Thus, a section of Keralites who benefitted from the expansion of education there could migrate to other Indian states or outside the country. Their economic or income status has improved despite inadequate economic opportunities in their homeland. There could be remittances from such migrants, and this could nurture a money-order economy there. However, all sections of people cannot migrate, and this may have implications for their welfare. This is especially so for people who are less educated, who lack financial or social capital to migrate, or those who face social restrictions in terms of mobility (say, women due to gendered social norms).

Even if the under-class party functions in a formal democracy, it may try to establish a 'party society', as noted by the political scientists in the case of West Bengal (when it was ruled by the Communist Party; Bhattacharyya, 2009; Chatterjee, 2009). This situation is not conducive to good governance. People may have to align visibly with the ruling party to get the benefits or goods transferred from the state. The services by the state including law and order could become a subject of intermediation at the level of citizens (in deciding who should get the service and who should not get) by the local unit of the ruling party or coalition. They would be able to continue with the rule as long as they could ensure the backing of the majority of voters (and also through some coercive practices during the elections). Under-class parties need not be ideologically committed to liberal democracy, and hence they do not have any internal incentives to work towards such a situation.

Modernisation by Under-Class Parties and Comparison with Social Counter-Elite Capture

The counter-elite capture by a party representing the under-class has some advantages over that by social counter-elites. Social identities are often along caste or religious lines. Thus, the states captured by any one group may favour their own people (with the same identity) at the cost of others. Or there could be an attempt to impose their religious values. However, historically, most underclass parties have adopted some versions of Marxism, and they have stuck to a secular polity. But there could be a forceful imposition of non-religious values or a suppression of the religious aspirations of the people. This may have some benefits if the suppressed religions or social groups were nurturing certain norms and values that are against some sections of the society, such as the women or those who do not follow or belong to their religion or group. (However, such religious values may not disappear completely even under a long-standing communist rule. Thus, people may get back to the church after the collapse of communist rule. Or patriarchal values may get strengthened once the grip of the Communist Party declines, as we have seen in a few Central Asian countries.)

The attitude towards science, scientific temper and rationality could be another issue over which social counter-elite may differ significantly from an under-class party. Since social identities have evolved from traditions (drawn from feudal social relations), their relationship to science may be ambivalent. They may use science or technology for specific ends, such as winning a war or improving productivity, but this may not translate into a positive approach towards scientific rationality. On the other hand, the acceptance of science and rationality may encourage under-class parties to work towards modernisation, which in essence may not be very different from the experience of the Western developed nations. Thus, the communist parties while negating the role of liberal democracy of the West did not work against the modernisation of the society. This may manifest in individualised relationships, including that between men and women. Even when communist or socialist parties work within a framework of democracy, their mobilisation of the poorer sections and the working class could be based on secular grounds, and they would try to facilitate a modernisation process. In this regard, the impact of an under-class party could be different from that of social counter-elite capture as well, even if the former is not able to establish a totalitarian state.

The Problem with Under-Class Capture

Why do not people allow the under-class party to rule forever? Why should there be a transition to competitive politics? We have already talked about the impact of ideology on the economic policies or the management of economy. It is amply clear that a centrally planned economy is inherently problematic and cannot sustain, even if we discount the corruption and inabilities of the rulers. The information required for the efficient functioning of an economy cannot be generated and used within the central planning system. Similarly, most people respond to personal incentives. If there are opportunities to make personal gains at the cost of the society, many people may use them. Thus, a system which does not create adequate incentives that reward efficiency and penalise inefficiency may not sustain well. It is difficult to create such incentives or disincentives without the use of markets. Moreover, it is incorrect to presume that the leaders (decision makers in a centrally planned economy) would continue to be socially benevolent (dictators) all the time. There could be instances where their decisions are driven by their personal gains, and not by the concerns about the maximisation of the welfare of the society as a whole. Thus with a reasonable degree of confidence, one can argue that under-class party rule combined with centrally planned economy may not sustain. There are not many states of this kind existing today. North Korea is one example, which is costly for its own people (in terms of minimal private consumption). The need to have a highly militaristic state to maintain one party rule is costly not only to itself, but also for others. The situation in Cuba is changing, and the leaders there seem to have realised the need for a market economy.

But what if the under-class party uses market economy? What are the problems of one-party rule or lack of competitive politics then? There can be multiple responses to this question. First is from the view point of the people living within the system. Do they want to continue with one-party rule (with market economy) which may facilitate higher economic growth (and hence an increase in personal consumption)? This cannot be answered easily. This situation is closer to that in China today. Although there are dissensions here and there, one can see substantial popular support for the regime there. Or it may be incorrect to assume that the Chinese Communist Party continues to be in power through brutal suppression of all the dissent there. This does not mean that there are no demands for enhanced individual and political rights in China. But the success in economic growth or increasing private consumption for different sections of society seems encouraging many Chinese to be less concerned about the lack of multi-party democracy there. This could be the situation also in Vietnam where the Communist Party rules with market economy. Moreover, one-party rule could be seen as solving some coordination problems, facilitating the growth of the economy and private consumption in certain contexts. This may also encourage some sections of society to take a lukewarm attitude towards struggles for establishing multi-party democracy in contexts such as in China.

There could also be normative responses to the need for competitive politics. Similar to the corrective incentives or disincentives provided by the market for the economy, democracy could ideally provide such corrective signals for the polity. In the absence of such corrective signals, the rulers can make mistakes or take decisions that are personally beneficial, but costly to the society. It is not easy to establish such corrective mechanisms in the absence of democracy. Communist parties (such as the one ruling China) have attempted to establish these corrective signals through internal democracy of the party. However, centralised democracy of the communist parties did not work well in the Soviet Union, and the party became a mere tool in the hands of the top leader for a certain period. People waited for his death to raise criticisms. On the other hand, the Chinese Communist Party seems to be using internal democracy reasonably well these days. They are transferring power from one set of leaders to others without waiting for the death of the former. However, corrective signals provided by the democratic elections cannot be replicated through party democracy.

What about the under-class parties in democratic contexts? There could be different reasons why frustration among sections of people develops, and this could lead to the electoral defeat of the under-class party. It is obvious if the under-class party stops representing the interests of the majority. The so-called under-class represented by the party can become a minority if there is growing affluence. However, this is a rare situation. These parties, for some reasons, may focus on some sub-groups among the under-class (such as formal sector working class or those mobilised by trade unions), and may neglect the unorganised sections including the poor.

Even if the situation is democratic, if the under-class party remains in power uncontested (for reasons such as the lack of an effective opposition), then it may show the problems of a one-party rule. This has happened in the case of West Bengal where the left coalition ruled for nearly three decades. It is realistic to expect that some members of the leadership of ideologically driven under-class parties would be more concerned about their own interest, and not much about wider public interest.

However, even with a 'good' party and socially committed leaders, one-party rule will have problems. Or even such a one-party rule could be rather unstable in a democratic process. In order to understand this, we need to consider the political process in comparison with the economic market: the exchange of goods and services. In the latter, suppliers cannot be expected to have concerns about the welfare of those who demand goods in a market, and the consumers cannot be concerned about the welfare of the supplier. Hence, the welfare-enhancing decisions are arrived at in markets through their cooperative bargaining (including the exercise of exit option, that is, deciding not to buy goods from a supplier), and not through the altruistic concern for the other. To some extent, this operates in politics too. Even if the party is ideologically committed to the welfare of all people and the leaders are genuinely interested in social welfare, there could be problems when people do not have a choice. Let us take an ideal government for the sake of argument. The government takes the best decision and gives the maximum possible to each citizen. How does a citizen know that this is the best that he/she could get from the government? For the citizen, there is an information asymmetry to know whether the government is doing the best for him/her. Hence, he/she may genuinely ask for more. This is like bargaining for the price of a commodity. While quoting a lower price, the buyer does not have to worry about the cost of production or the potential loss to the supplier. The supplier is expected to say 'no' when it affects his interest. This is the way the problem of information asymmetry regarding the cost of production is solved by the consumer in a market. On the other hand, in one-party rule, there is no mechanism to moderate the higher expectation of the citizen from the government. Such unmet expectations lead to frustration and may manifest in (explicit or hidden) demand for changing the government. It may take violent or non-violent social disorder when they cannot exercise the option of choosing the government. On the other hand, in competitive politics, the citizen will try to get more from one or the other party, and gradually would get signals on what is feasible for any government and what is not. If this is the situation with the most ideal government, one can see the greater need for competition with not-so-ideal governments and parties (and most political parties are of this type).

The Threats to Under-Class Party Rules

There are many reasons why internal opposition can emerge within the countries ruled by under-class party. In situations where the elites and affluent continue to exist, there could be political mobilisation by them pooling together people having negative feelings about the ruling party. The ideology of modernisation that most communist or under-class parties are wedded to may create enemies among those social groups which want to preserve their identities—religious, caste, racial, ethnic, regional and so on. The civil unrests in Tibet and western parts of China are examples in this regard. Or the 'liberation struggle' carried out by the religious and caste groups along with the centrist political party against the communist rule in Kerala is another example. The gradual dissatisfaction with the provision of private and public goods by the under-class party may also help breed opposition if the situation permits. We could see many such political struggles in the erst-while socialist states. The emergence of a populist politician who could channelise the anger has led to the collapse of three decades long communist rule in West Bengal.

In addition to the internal troubles, there were also external pressures from foreign countries that encouraged the transition in socialist countries. What makes one country interested in 'pushing' another country towards democracy? An answer to this question is given in Box 4.1.

Thus, through the tumultuous route of internal dissensions pos-sibly aided by external forces, some countries or regions captured by under-class parties may move towards competitive politics or democracy.

Box 4.1:
Why Are Some Countries Interested in Exporting Democracy to Other Parts of the World?

A popular answer would be that some countries are ideologically com-mitted to democracy, and hence they want to export these values to others. Or that they want to help others, in an altruistic sense, to have democracy, which they consider the desirable state of affairs. These could be partly true. But imposing (strongly encouraging to adopt) democracy is a costly exercise. Thus, there should be some self-interest too in this affair of exporting democracy.

There are some cases where the lack of democracy in one country can be perceived to be harmful to the people of the democratic world. In fact, the spread of communism as an idea was perceived to be a threat to the sustenance of democratic countries. Lack of democracy or individual freedom in some countries was seen promoting desper-ate migration to the democratic world. The decision making in non-democracies may be affecting the democratic world. For example, a non-democracy may attack another country without being bothered about internal moderating forces. Of late, the high level of unemploy-ment and domestic problems (including the lack of democracy) are perceived to be creating terrorist networks, and these are also seen as harmful to the developed world. In essence, all these perceptions encourage the developed world to encourage non-democratic countries to adopt democracy so that they are not affected by these externalities. This could be one reason for exporting democracy.

(Box 4.1 contd)

(Box 4.1 contd)

Another important reason is to expand business or economic growth of the countries which export democracy. The closed economies of the non-democracies and the close relationships that exist between the state and enterprises in these countries may be seen as affecting the competitiveness of international business. Just like avoiding desperate migration, democratic countries may have an interest in seeing that inputs (including natural resources) 'locked' in these countries are traded in much more accessible markets. Or that they want the markets in the non-democratic world to be more open, providing greater business opportunities for the firms and investors in the democratic world.

Source: Author.

Political Transition in States Captured by Under-Class Parties

Although movement towards competitive politics (including democracy) is relatively easy from a stage of social counter-elite capture, it may not be so easy from under-class capture. Under the former regime, there would be some sections of the previously ruling elite or some other social groups who would continue to be politically active in society, despite the capture of the state by one social group. Thus, there are counter groups to mobilise the sections of people disenchanted with the ruling party. However, in a situation of under-class capture, especially when they come to exist through non-democratic means or when they establish (forcefully) one-party rule, there could be a decimation of other forces which could potentially become a rallying point for people's frustration. There could be a de-eliticisation of the previously ruling elites after the capture of the state by the under-class. The new rulers may not encourage the formation of political groups around social identities. There could be suppression of religious or ethnic organisations.

Hence, the breakdown of the state captured by the under-class in a non-democratic situation would be through some 'revolutionary' changes. Such changes may happen under different situations. There could be some division within the ruling formation, or there could be a demand for changes within the ruling regime. To some extent, this has played an important role in the breaking down of communist rule in the Soviet Union. There were demands for change in East European countries even earlier, but that was suppressed by the overwhelming influence of the Soviet Union. Hence, the disappearance of communist rule in the latter enabled the collapse of such rules in the former set of countries.

Even when the rule led by the Communist Party broke down in these countries, they did not move smoothly towards competitive politics. The destruction of (or the non-emergence of) other rallying forces under the communist rule could be an important reason. Hence, even when Russia became democratic formally, and it started electing its rulers democratically, there was a perception that it had not yet become adequately democratic. A number of regions which were parts of the Soviet Union came under autocratic regimes driven by one ruler or a family. Only a few East European countries could establish democracy reasonably well after their transition from communist rule. The tradition of democracy in these countries (as part of the general European tradition) before the establishment of communist rule could be an enabling factor there. There were bloody ethnic wars and fragmentation in some other ex-socialist East European nations, such as Yugoslavia.

If the internal demand for political change is not coming up adequately, one could see 'managed changes' in the economic system (and marginally in the political system) as we could see in China, Vietnam, Laos and to some extent in Cuba of late. It is not that there are strong demands within these ex-socialist nations to move towards a competitive democracy. Thus, one could see the not-so-democratic Russia and the one-party regime in China enjoying substantial popular support, despite encountering some internal dissentions. Thus, the movement towards competitive politics may be a tumultuous route for countries where the underclass has captured the state.

Transition of Under-Class Parties in Democratic Contexts

In regions where under-class parties (communist or socialist parties) came to power through democracy or where they could not establish one party democracy, the transition is relatively easier. However, these parties, due to their inherent nature, may attempt to establish a party society trying to create a political monopoly, and the transition from there could be difficult depending on their success in this regard. We could see two contrasting cases in India—one from Kerala and another from West Bengal.

The geographical and historical factors (including the historical trade connections, influence of Christianity and Islam, the colonial rule and the role played the local kings, social reform movements, etc.) have played a role in laying a foundation for relatively better human development in Kerala even before Indian independence. The socialists who were initially part of the INC and who became part of the Communist Party later mobilised small (tenant) peasants and agricultural workers (belonging to backward communities) and other sections of the working class there. This mobilisation helped enhancing the self-respect of the oppressed and vulnerable sections. Thus, the non-elite mobilisation in Kerala was carried out on a class basis by this party. This has led to a counter-elite capture of the state government in 1957.

The Communist Party came to power in Kerala through elections. During its rule, there were allegations of it trying to establish a party society through what the opponents called 'cell rule'— attempts to manage the affairs in each village, including that of the law and order machinery, through the party committees. This situation and other policies of the government which were aimed at helping their constituency antagonised different sections of society—the Christians who saw communist rule as anti-religious, the previously ruling elites and so on. They could rally around the centrist (and, to some extent, elitist in the sense that it represented the affluent sections of the society in Kerala) Congress. There was a popular agitation against communist rule under the leadership of these forces. There were also allegations of indirect support from the United States of America (Nossiter, 1982). Finally, the central government of India controlled by the Congress dismissed the communist-ruled state government in 1959. (From then onwards, the successive elections saw coalitions led by either the communists or Congress ruling Kerala.)

One could see a combination of modern and conservative forces fighting against the non-democratic traits of communist rule there. The West European values enshrined among certain sections of Christianity, the centrist Congress party, intellectuals interested in preserving individual freedom, etc. represented the 'modern forces', whereas the previous (caste) elites and landlords fought against the communist rule from a conservative platform. However, the combination of these forces combined with the then prevailing situation in the national and international political environment (that is, the perceived need to avoid the spread of communism) enabled the removal of the Communist Party (and its defeat in successive election). Thus, competitive politics could emerge despite the hold of the Communist Party in Kerala in the fifties.

On the other hand, the transition to competitive politics in West Bengal after the rule by the communists took a much longer time. This is partly due to the success of the Communist Party in establishing a 'party society' in the rural areas of the state. On the other hand, the communists were effectively countered in the urban areas throughout its rule. The centrist party (that is, the Congress) was not successful in developing a coalition countering the influence of the communists. Only after committing some gross mistakes by the Communist Party in alienating sections of rural voters (through land acquisition for industrialisation) and through the emergence of a populist leader (Mamta Banerjee) that a regime change could be brought about in West Bengal, that too after nearly three decades of continuous rule by the communist-led coalition. It is not surprising that the Communist Party of West Bengal was thrown out on the basis of struggles against forceful land acquisition.

Hence, the transition to competitive politics could be a difficult process from under-class capture, as evident from the experience of socialist countries and also that of West Bengal. The near-destruction of the potential forces which could emerge as opposition, the hold established by the under-class party over different levels of the society, popular appeal created by the distribution programmes, etc.—these could create barriers against transition to competitive politics.

5

Competitive Populism

We have already discussed the threats encountered by the states captured by the elites, social counter-elites and the under-class party. These include contestation between sections of elites too. These threats and contestations may gradually lead to a competition among different political formations. It is interesting to see how such competition in politics influences the provision of public and private goods, and governance.

Real competitive politics come to exist only when each of the two or more parties or coalitions that compete has a reasonable chance of coming to power. Hence, democracy or election by itself does not imply competitive politics, especially if one party consistently dominates others in terms of electoral outcomes. For example, the period during which the INC came to power at the national level and in a number of states successively without encountering a strong opposition cannot be termed as competitive politics in India. This was the case in West Bengal for nearly three decades when the Communist Party of India (Marxist) (CPM)-led coalition was in power uninterruptedly, even though this was through periodical elections.

Similarly, the fact that there exists competitive politics at the macro (national or state) level does not mean that elite capture or counter-elite capture has disappeared at all levels in a country. Even in a state where parties compete strongly, one can see villages ruled or controlled by elites or specific social groups or by an under-class party without much real competition. Hence, the problems of elite or counter-elite capture may persist in such villages or in the local governments. In order to have real competition in democracy, a significant section of the voters should be capable (and willing) to shift loyalty from one political party to another, if they perceive a need to do so. If political fragmentation is on the basis of identities that are not easily changeable (such as religion, caste, region, race), it may decelerate the emergence of real competitive politics. This is so because people with a particular identity may not have access to (or may not be willing easily to be part of) a political formation with a different social identity. In that case, one may see competitive politics at the macro-level, but with parties having monopoly control over sections of the electorate.

Although this chapter is about competitive politics, the title given here is competitive populism. This is based on an argument advanced here that competitive politics in its initial stages in a developing society is likely to take the form of 'populism'. A definition of populism is needed here. The conventional notion of populism in politics is linked to the practice where different classes in a society collude to advance some opportunistic interests. For example, the domestic capitalists and the working class can join together to advance protectionist (or nationalistic) economic policies. Such a practice was visible in a few countries of Latin America in the seventies (Wynia, 1984; Dornbusch & Edwards, 1991). However, the notion of populism used in this book is a slightly different one. In poorer or developing economies where competitive politics comes to exist, there would be a greater demand for the provision of private goods by the state using public resources (directly or through cash transfer schemes).[1] On one hand, political competition may manifest mainly in this provision of private goods or money, and populism is used to denote this state of politics. On the other hand, the competition among political parties to provide public goods (or to address market failure) and rule of law, with a minimal role for the state in private goods provision, (which could be limited to the basic needs of the poorer and vulnerable sections of the people) is reckoned as 'liberal democracy' in this book, and it is discussed in Chapter 6.

---

[1] This definition of populism is closer to clientelism discussed in political science literature (as in Kitschelt & Wilkinson, 2009). However, this literature does not differentiate between different strands of clientelism, say, under-elite captured and counter-elite captured states or in competitive democracy.

Compulsions of Competitive Politics and the Emergence of Populist State

Competitive politics would encourage each party or coalition to enhance its support base. What does this competition to enhance support base lead to? Each group is likely to amass resources from the society for distribution among its actual and potential support base. Such public resources may come from tax and non-tax resources. Since direct taxes are less likely to be adequate to provide adequate resources in such countries, there will be a greater dependence on indirect taxes. This would mean a higher level of taxation on private consumption of different sections of the society. A major part of the resources may come from publicly owned assets or through borrowings (which are to be borne ultimately by the future generations). The competition between the elite and counter-elite or different counter-elites or different parties would mean that the quantum and coverage of the distribution of private goods would go up. This competitive expansion of the provision of private goods by the state is the outcome of populism discussed here.

It is not only the traditional vote bank of the ruling party or coalition that benefits from the private goods distribution by the state under competitive politics. If the competition is tough, each party would try to expand its base by providing similar benefits to a wider section of the population beyond its traditional vote bank. The toughness of competition could be measured in terms of the difference between the shares of the votes captured by the competing parties. If this difference is small, it is obvious that the competing parties will try to get the support of even very small groups—say, those social groups which constitute a miniscule percentage of the population, small sets of people living in remote hinterlands, and also some minor sub-sections who may have some views contrary to the main support base of the ruling party. In the absence of such tough competition, the needs of such people may be neglected.

Sometimes each political party may try to communicate to the traditional voters of the other party that the former represents their real interest. Thus, a party representing the richer sections may try to convince the poor that they should indeed be supporting it (rather than the party claiming to represent poor). In that process, it may do something visibly to attract the sections of the poor. Or both the parties—those claiming to represent the richer and the poorer sections respectively—may target the middle class to enhance their support base. This is the essence of median voter hypothesis.

In such a situation, the needs of the median voter would become the focus of the electoral agenda of both the political formations. This, in the context of a developing country, would mean that the private goods demand of the median voter is given undue attention by the competing parties. (On the other hand, even though such an influence of the median voter can be there in a liberal democracy context too, the public goods and tax preferences of the median voter may be attracting greater attention. This issue is discussed in the next chapter.)

It is possible to have a situation where the private goods demand of the median voter has such a stronger influence that even the party which claims to represent the poor may give greater weight to the needs of this (smaller) set of voters, rather than the poor who may constitute 40 per cent of the society. We have seen cases in India and elsewhere in the developing world where the per capita transfer to the sections of the middle class for private goods, such as electricity and pipe water supply, is higher than the amount given to the really poor for their consumption of all the commodities (Santhakumar, 2008). (This is possible because not many poor people have access to electricity or pipe water supply in many parts of the developing world.)

A similar impact of the median voter can be seen on the party representing the affluent. Even if the party has a support base of, say, 40 per cent of the people and if this set of population is not much interested in getting more private goods but only an appropriate combination of public goods and taxation, this party too may be influenced more by the needs of the median voter, rather than the majority of its own followers. Thus, even if their core support base is not concerned much about getting money and subsidised private goods from the government, it may be compelled to set its electoral agenda focussing on median voters who may demand greater distribution of private goods.

The political divide in all developing societies need not be on the basis of economic class. For example, the competition between Dravida Munnetra Kazhagam (DMK) and Anna Dravida Munnetra Kazhagam (ADMK) in Tamil Nadu is not on the basis of the poor versus the affluent. On the other hand, in Kerala where two coalitions—namely, the United Democratic Front (UDF) and Left Democratic Front (LDF)—compete, the LDF has greater support among the poorer sections, whereas the upper middle class and richer sections vote predominantly for the UDF. The political competition in Uttar Pradesh (UP) is between different coalitions of social groups, with the Samajwadi Party (SP) focussing on backward castes and Muslims, whereas the Bahujan Samaj Party (BSP) is trying to stitch a coalition of the Dalits and Brahmins. The latter case also shows that competitive politics would encourage the parties to look beyond their traditional vote banks to strengthen their electoral positions.

What is the impact of this enhanced coverage of private goods distribution by the state due to competitive politics? It enhances the consumption of the ruled majority, and this can be beneficial for the economy as long as their low private consumption is a constraint on economic development. Thus, the constraints imposed on economic growth due to under-nourishment, illiteracy and ill health of a large section of the society may become less formidable at this stage. Hence, competitive populism may enhance the chances of achieving higher levels of human development. Human development takes into account educational achievements and demographic transition (more specifically increase in life expectancy), in addition to per-capita income. This improvement in human development could be due to the fact that competitive populism encourages the provision of basic food requirements (through public distribution system), school education and primary healthcare to the widest section of people. The achievement of higher indices of human development in relatively poorer economies, such as Sri Lanka, Costa Rica or the Indian state Kerala, in the seventies or in Tamil Nadu later indicates this possibility. This is discussed in a little more detail in the following section.

Competitive Politics and Human Development in a Few Indian States

Although an under-class party (Communist Party) captured the state government in 1957, Kerala had an accelerated transition to competitive politics within three years. In that sense, it is the first state to enter into competitive politics in India. From 1960 onwards, coalitions led by either the Communist Party or INC came to power in Kerala one after another in successive elections (barring one election conducted immediately after the emergency period in India in 1977). This is a clear manifestation of competitive politics. A relatively smaller set of people, who votes for the ruling party but becomes unhappy with the government during its tenure, votes for the opposition party or coalition in the subsequent elections.

When the communist parties came to power in the sixties, they implemented land reforms (albeit partially) and bestowed ownership rights on the landless people (mostly belonging to the scheduled castes) who were living in huts on the land owned by their landlords. This has enhanced the self-respect of these people and made them demanding or participating in governmental provisions of education and healthcare (Raj & Tharakan, 1983). The political mobilisation by the left parties has also helped different sections of people to demand the extension of public services to them (Ramachandran, 1997). Because of popular pressure, the Congress-led governments also continued with these support programmes or enhanced their coverage. The public distribution system was an integral part of these expanded government services.

The two coalitions are by and large divided along the class lines—with the Congress-led coalition representing predominantly the richer and middle class, while the CPM-led coalition capturing most of the votes from the lower middle class, working class and the poor. However, the strong competition has encouraged both the coalitions to be concerned about the median voter, which has been changing over a period of time. The Congress got support from certain sections of the poor too which perceived from time to time that they are not adequately reckoned by the CPM-led coalition despite its pro-poor stand.[2] The INC was proactive in organising or supporting the scheduled tribes.[3] Yet another group which belonged to the poor in Kerala in the sixties and the seventies was the fishing population (Kurien, 1995). A substantial part of them were converted into and mobilised by the Latin Catholic Church. They too had a comfortable relationship with the INC. Whether it is due to the linkages with the poor, or due to the need to get support from sections of the poor and the lower middle class, the Congress-led coalition also continued with programmes that extended individual-oriented benefits in Kerala. Hence, the predominant class position of one of the competing parties or coalition in a competitive democracy need not be a constraint in extending its patronage to other classes.

The median voter in Kerala belonged to the lower middle class sections for a fairly long time (Santhakumar, 2003). The poor and the affluent, both, constitute a minority within the state. Those who earned a stable income from the low/middle level government or formal sector jobs (including the position of teachers in private-aided schools) were parts of the lower middle class. Both the coalitions were careful in extending greater private benefits to these sections of the society (even at the cost of the really poor).[4] Some of these steps were beneficial for the wider society too. For example, the step taken by the first communist government to pay the salaries of the teachers of aided private schools directly (and, thus, enabling private school teachers to earn salaries and

---

[2] For example, the scheduled tribes, which comprise nearly 1 per cent of the population, and a section predominantly poor have perceived that the CPM does not represent them adequately. This could be partly due to the focus of the CPM on the lower middle class in general, and backward communities like the *Ezhavas*.

[3] The first minister in the Government of Kerala from the tribal community, and that too a woman, is from the INC.

[4] The fact that these government employees were organised through trade unions also might have helped them.

pensions equivalent to those of government school teachers)—a step driven primarily by the influence of the teachers' unions on the Communist Party—but a practice followed by the successive governments helped the expansion of schooling in Kerala. The appointment of these teachers was in the hands of private school managers. Since the teachers received government-level salary, people seeking jobs in private schools were willing to pay a sizeable bribe to the school managers. (There were many candidates with minimal qualifications for these jobs, and hence private school managers could give jobs to those who paid bribes without flouting the entry requirements. But the managers were not appointing people based on any proficiency in teaching among the applicants.) This bribe encouraged individuals and caste or religious associations to use political influence to get permits to start more such private schools. This has led to the starting of schools in almost all parts of the state. Each private school developed an interest in increasing enrolment since the number of teachers' positions was based on the number of children enrolled. Hence, private schools struggled to enrol children from all socio-economic backgrounds, and also to retain them.

All the efforts aforementioned resulted in the spread of school education to most regions, caste groups and classes which covered both boys and girls. The expansion of education for women had other positive impacts. Female education played an important role in reducing household size (or number of children) in a noncoercive manner in Kerala (Ratcliffe, 1978). Hygienic practices (including child delivery at hospitals) that help reducing infant mortality was popularised. This reduction in infant mortality combined with social campaigns encouraging small families influenced women, and through them the families. This led to a faster demographic transition in Kerala compared to other Indian states. All these contributed to a higher level of human development in Kerala.

Kerala witnessed this phase of competitive populism for the next 30–40 years. This has shaped the government policies which have contributed to what is called the Kerala Model. But this beneficial impact of competitive politics on human development is not at all unique to Kerala. Competitive populism in Tamil Nadu created somewhat similar impact on human development in a different way at later point of time. The emergence of 'Dravidian' politics and the anti-Brahmin agitations there could be seen as part of the (social) counter-elite struggle. However, after the capture of the state by the DMK, competitive politics emerged in Tamil Nadu due to the split within this party in the seventies—led by two personalities, namely, M. Karunanidhi and M.G. Ramachandran. Although this competition is not between the elites and counter-elites, the one between two mass-based parties led by two personalities (and with Jayalalitha taking over the party founded by M.G. Ramachandran later) brought in bi-party competitive politics within this state. As an outcome of this process (and also the transition to social-counter capture earlier), the governments there have started adopting effective public policies that have helped in recording higher human development. Mid-day meal schemes have attracted more kids to school and also helped retaining them in classes (Prabhu, 2001). Family planning schemes, although these were somewhat supply-driven and top-down, met with success in the eighties and nineties. Higher levels of economic growth and increased tax revenues available to the state, combined with the competitive populism of the two main contending parties, led to a large number of schemes that transferred money or benefits to the poorer and vulnerable families. Over a period of time, one could see an expansion of private goods distributed—for example, cycles to girls, television sets, laptops, computers and so on. Hence, the experience of Tamil Nadu shows what a state would do in terms of achieving human development with public policies in a situation of competitive politics.

The fact that competitive populism helps enhancing expenditure in the social sector is evident from the experience of other Indian states as well. Andhra Pradesh entered into the phase of such populism after N.T. Rama Rao (NTR) came to power in the eighties against the then existing dominance of the Congress party, and after which both these parties started to rule the state. To some extent, the rise of the BJP or its alliance partners, such as the Shiva Sena in Maharashtra and Karnataka, too have accelerated the shift towards competitive populism in these states. All these have encouraged greater expenditure in the social sector or the subsidised provision of private goods and services to a wider section of population in these states. For example, free distribution of electricity to farmers (not only for those who have small size plots, but also even to those owning bigger stretches of land) is one such example. The populist competition between two elite-controlled parties can also result in the expansion of private goods provision to the electorate. However, it need not take care of the human development needs of all sections of the population, and may concentrate on the needs of the better off among them. Although the competitive populism between the Congress and BJP has helped in expanding the provision of free power to the farmers or the expansion of similar schemes, it has not led to a substantial improvement in the human development index initially in a number of states where such competition is strong.[5] However, this may happen over a period of time through the sustained competition of even two elite-controlled parties.

One can also consider the case of West Bengal in comparison with Kerala and Tamil Nadu. Kerala and West Bengal both had a long history of social and political movements which helped the mobilisation of the less-privileged sections (counter-elites) of society on a class basis. The Communist Party came to power in West Bengal in the seventies. Although the emergence of communist-led rule through alternate elections helped achieving higher levels of human development in Kerala, the uninterrupted communist-led government (for nearly three decades) did not lead to a substantial improvement of the human development index in West Bengal. (It may be noted that both these states faced challenges in terms of industrialisation, partly driven by the political and trade union mobilisation led by the left parties. These states have also been facing challenges in mobilising enough tax resources to meet the increasing public expenditure.)

There can also be a comparison between West Bengal and Tamil Nadu. West Bengal could implement land reforms reasonably well. Although there are social movements covering middle-caste

---

[5] To some extent, this is evident from the experience of Karnataka or Gujarat.

groups, Dalits continue to face certain degree of exclusion in rural Tamil Nadu. The state of Tamil Nadu did not face challenges in terms of industrialisation, and it is probably one of the states which attract higher levels of industrial investments. It could also mobilise substantial tax resources. The successive governments of Tamil Nadu used these tax resources and implemented certain social-sector programmes (albeit in a top-down manner), such as the mid-day meal scheme, and all these enabled them to achieve higher levels of human development in a relatively shorter period. The competitive politics in Tamil Nadu has encouraged each party to offer a wider set of resources to households (especially those who are below poverty line), and this has helped the process of enhancing human development there. Compared to Tamil Nadu and Kerala, the absence of competitive politics (until recently) could have worked against the achievement of higher levels of human development in West Bengal.

The failure of West Bengal under the left regime in terms of human development does not seem to be due to the inabilities in implementing redistribution policies or transfer schemes. For example, the state did reasonably well in terms of land distribution to the erstwhile tenants (Bardhan et al., 2009). Moreover, the provision of private goods or services was such that the state experienced serious fiscal difficulties compared to Kerala or Punjab. (The sluggish growth of the state economy/investments/the absence of remittances to the tune of Kerala may also have aggravated this situation.) However, the dominance of one party, especially at the grass-root level, could have limited the political choices of the people. This may manifest in different ways. First, some sections of people who may not align with the party visibly or who are not liked by the local party bosses may not have benefitted much from the provision of private goods and services (Bardhan et al., 2009). (Or such people may have encountered greater difficulties in accessing such public provisioning.) Secondly, in any setting, there would be people who may not like specific government policies, or there could be others who may encounter greater losses as the outcome of a governmental action. (It is possible that some people may encounter losses even if the policies or actions are efficient from the social point of view.) Such losers need genuine democratic forums to express their anger or frustration, and also to push their demands for higher levels of compensation. A political situation dominated by one party at the grass-root level may not provide adequate space in this regard. (Such a coercive environment could be seen in socialist states too, which have tried to improve human development through one-party rules. China required the forceful imposition of one-child policy to bring about the reduction in family size and the advancement of demographic transition.) In summary, even if the ruling party represents a wider section of the society, lack of competitive politics may inhibit actions that could lead to higher levels of human development in a non-coercive manner.

Impact of Competitive Populism on the Distribution of Public Goods

The distribution of private goods to wider sections of the society driven by competitive populism may have a negative impact on the provision of public goods. Quality of certain goods and services provided by the state may decline. This could be due to the combination of the following factors: (a) Competitive politics would encourage the state to expand the access to goods and services (which have some feature of public goods) provided by the state to wider sections of the society. This is usually achieved through subsidised pricing or not pricing at all. (b) Given the needs of providing private goods and also the subsidised expansion of other goods and services, there may not be enough resources to increase the quantum of public goods. Although electricity is provided free of cost or at highly subsidised rates to many people, the quality of power supply available in the grid could decline. Thus, states like Tamil Nadu which have enjoyed quality power supply in the past (with minimal duration of power cuts or interruptions) started encountering long duration cuts and interruptions. The state's ability to invest and generate more electricity to cope up with the increasing demand (which is driven partly by the administratively kept low tariffs) suffered (Santhakumar, 2008).

The allocation of public resources for agriculture in Indian states is another example to demonstrate this point. Agricultural development may require the provision of some private goods (such as better quality seeds, fertilisers, pesticides). The economic rationale in providing public resources to them is that such provision may enable the farmers to get to know the benefits of these inputs (in the context where they practice subsistence agriculture with minimal levels of modern inputs). However, there is no economic rationale for the continued provision of such inputs at heavily subsidised rates. Agricultural development also requires the provision of public goods in the form of expanded irrigation coverage, better quality roads and other transport infrastructure, marketing facilities and so on. This is where there is a strong rationale for government investments (due to market failure). However, competitive populism may lead to an allocation of more resources for the provision of private goods needed for agriculture, with a consequent reduction in the availability of resources for public investments in the sector. This can have a negative impact on the growth of the sector.

There could also be an increase in the fiscal deficits or debt burden of some of the states as a part of competitive populism. This would have a negative impact on the consumption of the future generations. It is somewhat ironical that some of the backward states, such as Orissa (which are yet to see competitive politics to a significant extent), could continue with surplus or balanced budgets, whereas states with relatively higher human development, such as Kerala, Punjab and even Tamil Nadu, started facing serious fiscal difficulties as part of their competitive populism. There could be some unwillingness on the part of state governments to spend money (Isaac & Ramakumar, 2006) (and hence ready to keep balanced budgets), and such unwillingness disappears as the state experiences strong competitive democracy which then leads the state to deeper fiscal deficits or crises.

Governance and Service Delivery in Competitive Populism

There are a number of services that we expect from the government; for example, issuance of a birth certificate, a driving license, the permit for constructing a house at a particular site and so on. These services should be delivered ideally based on an objective criterion without exercising any discretionary power. Here, the expected role of the elected representative or the politician is to highlight the general problems that the citizens face in this regard, to work towards improving the service delivery across the board or to change the criteria in such a way to maximise the social welfare. If the politician plays this role, it is more like intervention in public goods. Then there is little scope for personalised service. However, the situation in a developing society could be somewhat different. The politician or the elected representative may function as the intermediary between the state and citizen in the delivery of these public services.

Such personal services may include not only the intervention for getting such certificates or permits timely from the government office for those people (who, otherwise, would have to spare significant amount of time to get the service), but also the distribution of welfare benefits, subsidy, licenses or permits to those who do not necessarily meet the requirements, etc. Such intermediation exists under elite capture, counter-elite capture, and also under the monopoly rule of the under-class party. In all these cases, the intermediation is by and large a monopoly—a citizen does not have other options if he/she cannot get the service from the representative of the ruling party.

In a situation where only those representatives belonging to the ruling party could help the citizens, people who elect a representative belonging to the opposition may suffer. Moreover, people who are known to vote for the opposition party would also suffer. Such a situation would limit political choice, and also would encourage people to align visibly with the ruling party (a feature of party-society mentioned earlier or a situation closer to the counter-elite capture). This indicates that the real competitive politics does not exist in these contexts. However, in a situation of real or advanced competitive politics, one can see a different picture. This is evident from Table 5.1 where the data from a survey conducted in the local governments of Kerala is summarised (CDS, 2009).

The data show that people tend to approach elected representatives (ER) belonging to both the ruling coalition and opposition to get service faster. Both the types of representatives could help people, although, as expected, the ruling coalition ER are in a slightly (but not significantly) better position to intervene. Majority of ER consider that people remember thankfully if they could intervene to get quicker service. A slightly (but not significantly) higher share of opposition ER thinks that direct approach is better. This may be a reflection of their marginally lower ability to influence employees in the government offices, as they belong to the opposition. However, the overall picture is that people could use

Table 5.1:
Comparing Responses of Elected Representatives Belonging to Ruling Coalition and Opposition

Question	Total Percentage of Positive Response	Positive Response from the Ruling Party ER	Positive Response from Opposition ER Party	P Value
Do people approach you to get quicker service from the office?	85.20	86.49	83.87	0.432
Could you help them to get service quicker?	85.42	87.41	84.64	0.39
Will they remember thankfully your intervention?	70.10	70.94	69.26	0.68
Do you think that they should approach the office directly?	48.91	47.19	50.67	0.43

Source: Centre for Development Studies (2009).

ER belonging to both the ruling coalition and opposition to get quicker service from the local government. This reflects the situation of real competitive politics in Kerala. It could be the case that in most local governments (barring a small share), both the coalitions have a fair chance to be the ruling party. Even if this is not the case, both of these coalitions have almost equal chances to be the ruling party at the state level. The party ruling the state (or politicians belonging to this party at different levels) has direct and indirect ways of influencing the functioning of a local government, even if it is ruled by the other party. Thus, the employees of local government (who have to provide services, such as issuing birth certificates) not only consider the recommendation of the elected representatives of the party ruling the local government, but also those representatives representing the opposition. This is so because the party sitting in opposition, even if it cannot become the ruling party in this local government, it could be (or can become) the ruling party at the state level.

This situation has implications for the political choice of people at the local level. First of all, even if the person they vote for fails in the election to the local government (and even if their voting preference is known to the person who is elected), they do not have to fear serious repercussions. Secondly, similar is the situation even if the person for whom they have voted won, but his/her party failed to secure the majority in the local government. This is so because the person failed (or his party colleagues who have won) or the party sitting in opposition also have some influence in the local government. Even after voting for, if a citizen develops an adversarial relationship with a specific ER, this too cannot deprive him/her much from 'personalised service' from the local government, since he/she has the option to approach other representatives of the same party or those belonging to the other party.

This is more like a competitive intermediation, compared to the monopoly intermediation under the elite or one-party rule led by counter-elites or the under-class. Such competitive politics could be liberating, relatively at least. Under this form, people do not have to be in the 'good books' of the local elite or counter-elites who capture the state, or to be the open votaries of the ruling party.

Either their money (which could be used to pay bribe) or their votes become a reward to buy the services of the politician. There may be an element of choice for the citizens in terms of individuals within a party or across the party. Thus, competitive politics may be reckoned as an improvement in terms of governance over other political regimes as discussed in the previous chapters.

Competitive politics can bring about a change in the way people deal with political representatives. If strong party loyalties and active participation in the political mobilisation for or against the ruling coalition are the characteristics of politics in other regimes, probably this gradually makes way for individuals to use politicians of different parties to get different (private) benefits from the government as part of competitive populism. In one sense, this amounts to the 'de-politicisation' that many radical scholars are concerned about (Hout, 2008). In another sense, the politician transforms himself/herself in this context to an agent which is acceptable within a liberal democracy or an economics framework of principal–agent relationship. However, this transformation becomes problematic in competitive populism because the politician–citizen relationship gets 'trapped' in the provision of private benefits or goods, whereas the expected role of the politician as an agent (in liberal democracy) for the provision of public goods for the citizens is not getting realised adequately.

As noted earlier, competitive politics leads to the expanded provision of private benefits or services to the people. This may reduce the incentives of the elected representatives to improve governance. In this context, there is a need to define what we mean by an improvement in governance. We may consider different activities of a government and the role of improved governance in that regard. This is summarised in Table 5.2.

For poverty eradication schemes, an improvement in service delivery (or governance) would mean that all the poor people should get the specified help or support without much delay. This would require a reasonably objective criterion for deciding or identifying the poor, and also an effective mechanism to extend support to such people without delay. With respect to service delivery in general (say, the issue of certificates or permits), improvement

Table 5.2:
Improvement in Governance and the Disincentives of ER

Governance Activity	Improvement Indicator	Incentive of ER
Poverty eradication or social support	All the poor get adequate support without delay and discrimination	Discrimination
Service delivery	Provide quicker service to all who meet requirements	Sustain a situation to help some
Overall resource allocation	Provide adequate public goods; minimise the provision of private goods	Provision of private goods
Direct support to the non-poor	Use sparingly if wider social benefits are ensured	Liberal with private goods provision

Source: Author.

in governance would lead to the provision of such services in minimum needed time to those who meet the well-known requirements. Here, good governance would also mean that those who do not meet such requirements will not get the service (that is, permit or certificate). In terms of the overall resource allocation of a government, an improvement in governance would lead to the provision of adequate public goods to all, and support for private goods to those who are really in need (like the poor and other vulnerable sections). This is not to say that there should not be any private goods provision or direct support to the non-poor. A good government would do this sparingly when there are clear social benefits.

When we take the improvements in governance in each of the activities as in Table 5.2, politicians operating in competitive populism do not have enough incentives to work towards such improvements. For example, if the poor are identified on the basis of an objective criterion and if they get the support from the government office without delay, the scope of personal service by the politician gets minimised in this regard. Hence, they are less likely to work towards such reform. Similar disincentive to improve the system exists in the case of the subsidy provision. There can be a higher level of discretion on who requires (who does not require) subsidy, especially when such subsidy would benefit the non-poor.

For example, a government can decide to provide subsidy to coconut or cashew growers without worrying much about the relative wealth status of such growers. Thus, any improvements in governance leading to an objective criterion, here, is likely to reduce the scope of personal servicing for the ER.

The scope for personalised service will be narrowed if greater amount of public resources is allocated for the public goods. This is so because such goods benefit all in a given situation, and not necessarily those who support this elected representative. He/she cannot exclude the non-supporters (or 'enemies') from using such goods and services. This reduces his/her incentives to argue for allocating a greater part of public resources for public goods. Regarding service delivery, the key improvement in governance is to be able to provide services to all those who are seeking them, provided they meet the required criteria. It is here that the use of information technology for the easier and effective storage of documents/data/information, and also for the quicker retrieval and processing, is relevant. However, such quick delivery for all citizens minimises the scope for providing personalised service by the ER. If they perceive personal servicing to be too important a factor in enhancing their re-election probability or for building up their political capital, they may not have the incentive to improve the service delivery mechanism. This may work as a disincentive for the speedy implementation of effective e-governance.

Considering all these functions of governance and the indicators of improvement in governance, one can see that ER (or politicians in general) operating within a context of competitive populism (or competitive politics in a poorer or developing society) do not have adequate incentives to work towards better governance.

Competitive Populism and Capitalist Growth

Competitive populism is likely to upset the relatively 'comfortable equilibrium' in terms of capitalist or industrial development under elite or counter-elite capture or the state-led industrialisation in a situation of under-class party capture. The close connection between the elites and a section of capitalists that may have existed under elite capture and which may have facilitated certain level of undisputed capitalist development is one such equilibrium. This was disturbed with the counter-elite capture. However, counter-elites who capture power may also establish their own comfortable relationships with capitalists, or they may become elites in due course as a part of 'crony capitalism'. Under-class parties may take over all enterprises and bring them under state (or essentially under party) control. All these symbiotic relationships between the state and capitalist or productive enterprises would be challenged under competitive politics.

It is not that either the elite or the counter-elite who survive under competitive politics (or different political parties representing them) will not try to re-establish such close relationships with capitalists as they come to power through competitive politics. They would try it hard indeed. But this may create protests from the opposition and allegations of corruption (whether real or fictitious), and these may persuade a section of the population. This does not need an opposition which is ideologically against a close relationship with the capitalists. They may even argue for such a relationship, but would see the one entertained by the party in power as corrupt. It is obvious that there are strong interests for the political party sitting in opposition to raise such allegations whether these are really true or not. However, such allegations may discourage the ruling party from going ahead with such cosy relationships with the capitalists, if these can persuade an electorally important section of the population.

This would have an impact on capitalist development. It is true that capitalist investments require a facilitating institutional environment. In modern democracies, such institutional environment is provided by formal institutions which have a set of rules which are generic in nature. For example, any investor may have to follow certain rules, and once he/she follows these rules, he/she would get the protection from the rule of law, even without establishing any close relationship with the specific arms of the state or its apparatuses. However, such formal institutions do not exist or do not function well even if they exist in developing economies. Thus, the facilitating institutional environment needed for the capitalists in such contexts is created through their close (sometimes personal) relationship with the state or its representatives. There could be cases of buying the state actors—which can take different forms starting from bribing an official issuing permit to the bribing of or capturing the ruler or ruling party. Capitalist development requires such close relationships in the absence of an enabling institutional environment through well-functioning formal institutions. (One need not see such close relationships as corrupt or 'immoral' in all the contexts. For example, the economic growth in East Asia or in China is driven partly through such close relationships. There can be a non-corrupt ruler who entertains such close relationship with the capitalists to usher in higher levels of economic growth in his/her country.)

This route of capitalist development may be affected under early stages of competitive politics, if allegations of corruption in the relationships between ruling party and capitalists can become an important electoral issue (potentially causing frequent regime changes). This was an obvious issue in the state of Kerala. However, until recently, the ruling regimes in Tamil Nadu did not face such a problem. Not many voters in that state were willing to throw out a regime due to allegations of corruption against the ruling party. (There may be a change in that situation as evident from the elections held there in 2010.) Thus, if there are enough swing voters to cause a regime change, who would be persuaded by the allegations of corruption in the relationship between the state and capitalists, it would have a negative impact on the capitalist development in that context. This problem could be solved only gradually through the development of well-functioning and impersonal formal institutions mediating the relationship between the state and capitalists, and this may take time. Thus, it should not be surprising if there is a downturn visible in the case of capitalist development (and hence economic growth) in societies witnessing an early stage of competitive politics.

If we see certain situations where capitalist development takes place through close relationships with the ruling regimes in formally democratic situations (say, in the case of Tamil Nadu a few years ago, or that of Gujarat), this could be due to one of the following two reasons: (a) Though there exist formal democracy, competitive politics is yet to take root in reality; there could be a relatively uncontested dominance of one party there; there could be many sub-contexts here which sustain the features of elite or counter-elite capture; (b) Despite the existence of competitive politics, it has not thrown up a section of the population which is willing to vote out a regime, even if there are allegations of corruption. The latter can happen if the majority of voters are concerned only about the private goods transfer that they get from the state or in preserving the patronage relationships with the landlords or specific capitalists. It may take time to change this situation, and it requires the emergence of a class interested in the competition between different capitalists. This is discussed in detail in the next chapter which deals with liberal democracy.

The competitive politics between the elite and counter-elite or different political parties may result gradually in a certain level of competition between different capitalists. Even the competition of the capitalists to be in the company of either the elite or the counter-elite, who are competing with each other, could be beneficial to some extent. Thus, the social loss associated with crony or monopoly capitalism is likely to decline, albeit, marginally in such politically competitive societies. However, if the lack of enough political competition is an important incentive for making investments, such investments may come down as part of competitive politics. This may also depend on other avenues for capital investments. If there are nearby locations where 'monopoly rents' are possible, that could be an important reason for avoiding locations sustaining competitive politics. This rent need not be derived from product markets alone. These may be available from input or factor markets too. Land or labour may be made available at cheaper rates where crony collaboration with the state is possible. Labour can be made cheaper if the state helps in reducing the trade union bargaining power of the employees. These too may encourage capitalists to favour locations (in developing world) which sustain lesser political competition, and it may have a decelerating impact on economic development in places with higher levels of competition. Like the possible decelerating impact of competitive populism on capitalist development, there can be a negative impact on the implementation of growth-oriented economic reforms. This is discussed in detail in Santhakumar, 2008.

Corruption under Competitive Populism

We have already argued that the distribution for private goods to the population is the prime role of the government in this phase, and competitive democracy would mean that each ruling party or coalition will try to extend the coverage of this distribution. This may encourage the governments to extract a greater part of the resources, and use it for such distribution. This by itself cannot be called corruption. However, as noted in the counter-elite capture, such taxing may not be carried out only by the government. There can be a decentralisation of 'taxing' at the lower levels of political and government functionaries. Competitive democracy would also ensure that there will be compulsions not to disturb the different constituencies which benefit directly or indirectly from such informal taxation. Moreover, if majority of the people are poor or if their incomes are lower, their demand for public goods could also be low, and thus there may not be any serious concern about breaking the rules regarding those public purposes.

However, the most important factor that moderates corruption is competition itself. Strong competition provides incentives for the opposition party to highlight the 'corruption' of the ruling party. However, this makes an impact only when the significant sections of the electorate see corruption as an issue to vote governments out of power. It may take some time for such a section of population to emerge in competitive democracies. Until then, both the ruling and the opposition parties may indulge in corrupt ways to keep their support base happy (and to make inroads into the support base of the other), even though they may pay lip service against the corruption of the other. This is primarily because the majority of voters do not see corruption as a serious issue, and they want the governments to give them private benefits, even if through corrupt means.

There are two major related issues here. Public goods demands for the majority of population may continue to be low, and this may have an impact on the incentives to control corruption even under competitive democracy. Thus, many voters may not see the costs in terms of lost public goods while seeking more private goods from the government. Secondly, the direct tax base in such societies could also be limited. The quantum of indirect tax paid by substantial sections of the society could also be lower, if their market-based private consumption is also lower (and if there are tax concessions for essential commodities like food). Thus, many may not perceive the tax costs (or the need to pay higher taxes) due to their demand for more transfer from the government for private goods consumption.

The citizens' relationship with politicians (or political parties) is to get maximum private benefits (through private goods) from public resources. Given the divisibility and excludability of such resources, each individual (or group) is in a competition with others to extract maximum from the public kitty, and each politician is in competition with the other politician to provide maximum resources to the relevant electorate so that his/her political objectives are met. The relationship between the politician and the electorate is personal. The rules made for maximising social gains (in situations of market failure where isolated individual actions need not maximise social gains) could be an obstruction for the transactions between individuals and politicians for mutual personal benefits (especially so because politicians, who are part of these transactions, are also the ultimate enforcers of such rules). Thus, breaking rules which are made for maximising social gains need not be seen as a serious issue. Recommending the tweaking of a rule or to break the queues to provide (sometimes not so eligible) benefit to one individual or a group need not be seen as a serious violation by the politicians. This is known to the government officials too. They can also do the same by taking bribes from the individual beneficiary (since they do not have political gains). Politicians do not have the incentive to control discretionary powers currently being misused, as they too benefit personally from such powers. Electorate, at large, is also interested in not having transparent eligibility conditions and priority rules, since they too wish to get the maximum benefit through personal relationship with the politician (and do not want these rules to be a hindrance to the attainment of their personal gains).

There may not be adequate demand for enforcing rules (or to avoid corruption) from the society under this stage of competitive democracy. Thus, being corrupt need not be seen as a major disqualification for a politician to throw him/her out of power. Thus, it is not surprising to see politicians known to be corrupt (or against whom legal cases are filed) winning elections with thumbing majority in elections in countries, such as India.

We have talked about corruption in the day-to-day transactions with the politicians or government offices. What about big-ticket corruption in competitive populism? Usually such big-ticket corruption happens in the transactions between industrialists and politicians. There may be an interest in opposing this corruption for the opposition parties and for the electorate at large, if the latter do not see any benefit from such corrupt dealings. However, there are channels through which the gains from corruption can flow downwards in politics. First of all, such gains can be redistributed within the party organisation to the lowest level, and this can keep party machinery well oiled. This may also enable the party functionaries to continue with the 'provider role' for sections of the electorate. The big-ticket corruption at the macro level and the incentives provided by this to the government may also facilitate private investments, and the resources mobilised from such investments, legally and illegally, by the state and the political machinery may be used to provide private goods to sections of the society. This interest in getting private benefits may encourage substantial sections of the electorate to set a blind eye on the kickbacks received by the ruler or ruling party through the facilitation of such investments. These factors too may dampen the social opposition to corruption in competitive populism.

Competitive Politics and Media

Competitive politics can enhance the competition between different media firms. Competing political formations may have direct or indirect control over media firms, and this could be one reason for the sustenance of competing media there. In addition, capitalists also may be interested in investing in media. Due to the non-tradable nature of media, investments in local media would be profitable even if investments in tradable goods and services are not so profitable due to the cheaper imports. Hence, a capitalist who is not so much interested in investing in manufacturing of tradable commodities in a setting due to higher costs may be interested in investing in media and related services. The competition in politics will also spur competition in discourses, ideas and ideologies, and these may facilitate the emergence of multiple products in media with different newspapers, different TV channels, etc., nurturing or supporting different ideas. Moreover, the presence of a powerful opposition party, which has a reasonable chance to come to power, may prevent the possible oppression of the freedom of the media (and journalists) by the ruling regime. This is a necessary condition to enable journalists to unearth the corrupt deals of the representatives of the ruling regime.

Let us assume that such a society has two media houses—both owned by the industrialist class. However, the competition within media itself may encourage each one of them to support one or the other political group or voices competing in politics. For example, if the government is controlled by an elite party and the opposition by a counter-elite party, one can see one media supporting the ruling regime whereas the other backing the opposition. Here, one need not view the interest or the agenda of a media firm in a moralistic manner. Each media channel may have an interest in bringing out scoops and investigation stories that catch the widest attention of the readers as possible. This may even cause real and fictitious stories of corruption to be in the public domain causing heartburns to even some genuine or non-corrupt politicians.

As noted earlier, newspapers (or TV channels) are also like political parties. They may have traditional readers (such as the traditional vote banks of the parties). Media needs to enhance the subscriber base. Unlike the case of other products or services, one customer is likely to buy only one copy of the newspaper, and hence expansion of operations would require widening of the subscriber base. Even for advertisement revenue, such widening is important. Thus, the need to reflect the interest of sections of subscribers is paramount in a competitive media space. Driven by the urge to expand business, each media channel may try to attract the traditional readers of others. This may create situations similar to the median-voter dominance in bi-party political competition. Hence, even if one media channel (say a newspaper) represents a particular personal/class interest/ideology, the competition to acquire more subscribers may encourage it to dilute its own interest/ideology, and to respond to or reflect more 'popular' ones.

The circulation of stories by the media and its reuse by the political parties in competitive politics may create a situation which makes the close relationships between capitalists and ruling regime unsustainable. Competitive media may make frequent regime change possible. But competitive media can also play a positive role in terms of human development as noted by Amartya Sen (Sen & Dreze, 1989). He noted the role of media in highlighting the situations of extreme deprivation, such as famine, encouraging the state machinery to act. Although the media is more likely to highlight newsworthy shocking incidents such as disasters, there will be some attempt to highlight manifestations of underdevelopment such as malnutrition, illiteracy or drop out from schooling, infant mortality and so on. These may encourage competing parties to take up these as political issues and a ruling party (fearing failure in elections in a highly competitive politics) to take effective steps. However, it need not be the benevolence of the media or the journalists that make them highlight such stories of deprivation. The competition among them and the need to enhance their market share may encourage them to highlight such stories in a manner that catches maximum attention of the society.

In that sense too, competitive populism and competitive media have similarities. We have seen that competitive populism is likely to encourage social spending that may lead to improved human development indicators as compared to a situation where such competition does not exist. This is irrespective of the ideological position of the political parties. Similarly competitive media with a deepened subscriber base may work towards better human development, irrespective of the class or ideological position of their owners.

The politics that makes different social groups to support or oppose a specific government would also influence the media. Hence, if a media firm opposes a specific government, it need not be due to reasons of social welfare. Such opposition is more likely as some social group opposes the government (or its specific policies), and hence this particular media wants to capitalise on this opposition. In this way, the different interests played out in competitive populism will also shape the public discourses sustained by the media.

Hence, if a section of the society wants more public resources to be provided as private goods (or transfer for the consumption of such goods), the competing media may highlight this demand. They may share the demands of the competing social groups, each of which wants to enhance the size of the public-resource cake for their private consumption. Even if the owners of the media come from elite sections, who are likely to have higher demand for public goods, media owned by the elite cannot truly represent the trade-offs of the elites in this regard. They may have to argue for greater transfer of resources for private goods consumption, even when that may have a dampening effect on public goods provision demanded by the elite who owns the media.

The competition between different media houses may have an impact on corruption too. The media which develops an interest in opposing a government (due to its interest in sustaining a subscriber base) has an interest in unearthing some of the corrupt deals of the government even when the media or the groups owning it has no fundamental opposition to corruption. The subscribers who like such stories of corruption need not have any fundamental opposition to corruption, but they are likely to dislike the corruption benefitting others. However, there can be certain situations where even an oppositional media may not be interested in bringing out the corruption deals of the government. Some of these are: (a) when the media house or its owner benefits directly from the corruption; (b) when an individual journalist colludes with the beneficiaries of corruption and such collusion is not uncommon; and (c) there can be instances where associations of journalists or media houses may get into deals with the government that benefits all their members. Even though the other media firms may have an interest in bringing out corruption of type (a), they may be discouraged by the collective interests of the media. There can be some collusive strategies not to reveal the benefits that each media directly receives from the state, since every media firm may be getting (or hoping to get) similar benefits from the political establishment. However, competitive media provides enough space for bringing out a substantial set of corruption cases into the public sphere. The way the public responds to such media stories on corruption (and, hence, to some extent the interest in bringing out corruption stories for the media) depends on the incentives of people to take a position against corruption. This is discussed in detail in the next chapter.

In summary, the emergence of competitive politics and populism is an important phase in political transition. This helps achieving human development. There could be some negative impacts on the provision of public goods and on economic growth or development as part of the populism. However, attempting to achieve economic growth without enhancing human development could be an unsustainable route, even if economic development is the only concern. Hence, we need to take a much more nuanced view on competitive populism.

6

Moving Beyond Competitive Populism

We have seen that the preponderance of the provision of private goods and individual-oriented services is the dominant feature of governance in competitive populism. In order to improve governance, there has to be a reduction in the role of such 'personal servicing' in the function of a government. How does it happen?

There are a number of difficulties in answering this question. First, one can see traces of competitive populism even in the developed democracies. For example, the logjam in decision making—one can see it not so rarely in the United States (US) Congress—over issues of taxation (whether to increase or decrease tax rate) for specific sections of the society is an indication that political parties fight over the distribution of public resources for private benefits (and not merely for the public goods) of their constituencies even in advanced liberal democracies. Secondly, among the developing countries currently sustaining competitive democracy, it is very difficult to identify the point at which these could be said to have moved out of populism.

What do we mean by saying that a society has moved out of competitive populism or has entered into liberal democracy? In order to address this issue, liberal democracy is defined here to have some specific features which include the following:

1. A larger part of the public resources is being used for providing public goods (including the rule of law valid more or less equally for all) or other goods and services as a way of addressing some issues of market failure.
2. Public money is spent for a viable social security or for the provision of private goods to only those who need it or only

at times when anybody needs it (based on a widely accepted social rationale).

3. Democracy may manifest in the following two competitions: the class or ideology-based parties competing over the quantum and coverage of taxes (or quantum of public resources); territorial representation leads to some competition for public goods among different territorial constituencies.

4. Politicians having an interest in across-the-board improvement in governance and public service delivery at times can be avoided. The delivery is expected to be quicker and to be on the basis of meeting certain well-known criteria, and it is not intermediated by the interventions of specific politicians for the benefit of specific individuals or citizens.

Interest of Different Classes or Groups to Get Out of Competitive Populism

From the political economy point of view, one can say that a country comes out of populism when politicians see the emergence of a class interested in liberal democracy (the way it has been already outlined), and is capable of influencing electoral outcomes. This is obvious if the majority of voters in a context are such that they demand liberal democracy. However, even without becoming majority, it is possible to have a class that can influence electoral outcomes. One possibility is through their position as the median voter, which we have discussed earlier. In specific situations of competitive democracy, median voter can influence electoral outcomes and the agenda of competing political parties. We have seen that the private goods requirements of this median voter could encourage the political parties to continue with competitive populism. It is possible that under certain other situations, the median voter may gradually become interested in the features of liberal democracy, rather than persisting with demands for populism. The emergence of such a situation is the focus of the discussion in this section.

There are different trade-offs encountered by different groups in society with regard to competitive populism. The emergence of a class interested in getting out of competitive populism should be analysed on the basis of these trade-offs. Let us consider some generic groups in this regard: the poor, the middle class and the rich.

The Poor

For the poor, they need public support for their consumption of basic private goods. For some reason, they are unable to acquire enough income from labour markets to buy adequate amount of basic goods and services, and that is why they are considered poor. Given their needs for private goods, they would (be compelled to) have a relationship with the politicians with the expectation of getting private goods. Since the provision of a unit of private goods to a person deprives the other from getting the same unit, the relationship of a specific citizen with the politician is personal. Hence, the poor are likely to enter into a patronage-seeking relationship with politicians or political parties. Such a relationship could be used not only for getting private goods, but also for mediating to get public service delivery or to get benefits of (or to circumvent) the rule of law. For example, the practice of seeking politicians' mediation to approach police station, either to get the services of the police as an affected party or to get a favourable treatment from the police as an accused is not at all uncommon in the villages of India. The demand for public goods by the poor is likely to be lower due to the positive correlation between the consumption of private goods and the demand for public goods. Hence, it is safe to assume that the demand for liberal democracy (the way it is defined here) is less likely to emerge from the poorer sections of the society.

The Rich

Let us consider the rich. The rich in the developing world are likely to be those who benefit from different kinds of rent. Either they may be getting rent from physical properties (such as land) or from monopoly business. Even otherwise, each industrialist wishes to have some monopoly, and hence competition is not in his/her own interest. Thus, they may seek to have some monopoly or restricted market competition through institutional or policy measures. A direct relationship with politicians is one way of sustaining or acquiring this monopoly. Hence, the rich are likely to expect a personalised service from the politician or the expectation from the politician is not to provide any across-the-board 'opportunities to compete' or a level-playing field to everybody. Moreover, industrialists would be in a better position to get the personalised service of politicians (even for getting a license from the government quickly) on payment or other kinds of direct rewards. Their demand for public goods, which is likely to be higher due to their higher incomes, could also be communicated to the political class through such direct relationships. Moreover, some among the richer sections, such as industrialists or traders, may have organised lobbying activities, and these too enable their direct communication with the politicians. They may be a major contributor to the taxes of the treasury, but through close contacts with the politicians, they may either ensure that they get higher rents (through limited competition) and/or that they get adequate public goods or other services from the state or that their taxes are not high. Closer and more personalised the service from the politician, the better for the industrialists. Thus, the richer sections need not have adequate incentives to demand across the board improvements in governance—a key feature of liberal democracy.

The Middle Class

What about the middle class? A greater part of the private goods consumed by the middle and upper middle classes cannot be provided to them by any government. For example, even if we take food, the middle class would be consuming different types (and quality) of food much beyond what could be provided through a public distribution system. Hence, their dependence on commodity markets would be much higher than that of the poor. In fact, such dependence on market of the middle class may be much higher in the poorer and developing countries. Even for schooling and health care, the quality of state-provided service in these countries could be woefully inadequate for their emerging middle class (whereas one can see the middle class depending more on publicly provided services of schooling and health care in the developed economies). Hence even when certain commodities and goods are provided by the state (at subsidised rates), the middle class may lose interest in them for 'quality' reasons (as perceived or desired by them). Thus, the provision of private goods, in general, by the state may become less attractive to them. Therefore, they have an interest in sustaining competition in or working against monopoly in commodity markets.

In general, the middle class is likely to save and invest some money in different financial instruments—bank deposits, bonds, mutual funds, shares and so on. An efficient functioning of the financial and capital market is in their interest. Manipulation by a capitalist in share market can be really harmful for these small investors. Hence, they may have an interest in appropriate disclosure of information, curbs on insider trading and other such regulations.

Although the middle class may enjoy certain monopoly in their current jobs, they are likely to demand competition in labour markets as well. This is so because they, as individuals, cannot do much to sustain that monopoly, and they are less certain *ex-ante* on the benefits of assigning monopoly (limited competition) to any particular occupation, as they are not sure of the job in which they or their wards may land up. Although sections of the middle class may be drawing rental incomes, a greater part of their income is likely to come from wages or salaries. For the competition in commodity or capital markets, a close relationship between politicians and capitalists, and the associated monopoly practices could be harmful to the middle class. Thus, they are likely to demand a political system where decisions are in favour of competition wherever these are in their interest, and there are many situations where they suffer from a lack of competition.

As the private consumption of sections of the middle class increases, there could be a corresponding increase in the demand for public goods in general. This is not a mere theoretical observation that the consumption of private and public goods is positively correlated or that the willingness to pay for public goods, at the margin, increases with the income of the people. When people start buying a motor bike or a car (private goods), the woeful conditions of the road and other infrastructure (public goods) become more noticeable, and they will start cribbing about them. When they start living in nicer apartments and housing complexes, lack of solid-waste management may become an issue of concern. However, their incomes are not so high to provide adequate quantity of such public goods on their own. For example, a millionaire may be able to construct a road to his house, whereas a typical middle class household may want such a road badly, but is unlikely to be able to construct it on its own. Thus, they want the government to provide public goods. Or the lack of adequate public goods could become more and more costly to them. If the inadequacy of the public goods is perceived to be driven by the need for allocating more of the public resources for the subsidised provision of private goods (for which the middle class has started depending more on markets), this could be a major reason for the decline of their support for populism. The demand for public goods for the middle class is higher than that of the poor, but the former does not have any close relationship with the politicians to communicate their needs directly or to get such goods in a personalised manner, unlike the capitalists.

The middle class is less likely to be part of lobbies to communicate their tax preferences directly to the politicians. The use of a greater part of tax resources for private goods is not to their liking, if that leads to an increase in the taxes that they have to pay. Thus, they may be interested in lower taxes and/or a comparable provision of public goods from the state. Regarding public service delivery, they may prefer quicker service delivery due to the higher opportunity cost of time. They may not have enough connections with the politicians to use their influence to get quicker services. They may not even want to have a paternalistic relationship with the politicians. The people who were poor or the lower middle class earlier and who have become part of the middle class currently, need not have nicer memories of the paternalistic relationship with politicians. It may be noted that the relationship of the politician with the poor is likely to be an unequal one with the dominance of the former. (On the other hand, the relationship of the politician with the capitalists or the rich is more likely to be on an equal footing.) The person emerging out of poverty may also want to get out of this unequal relationship. All these may discourage the middle class from establishing, or preferring to establish, a personalised relationship with politicians.

However, it would be wrong to assume that all sections of the middle class have an interest in demanding (or at all times or in all contexts) liberal democracy or related policies from the state. There may be services or sectors in which the middle class may be currently enjoying substantial cash transfer or subsidy from the government. They may not like the withdrawal of such subsidies. The case of electricity and water supply wherein a greater part of the subsidy is enjoyed by the middle class in many developing countries was mentioned in an earlier chapter. A similar situation is there in the case of petroleum fuels (such as petrol, diesel, LPG, etc.) in a number of countries. For example, the annual subsidy received for LPG by a middle class household in India (and only a few among the poor have access to this service in the country) would be equal to the pension given to an older person from a poor family, who does not have access to any formal social security. In such cases, the middle class may not be interested in removing subsidy, and may work against the competition in the provision of these services if subsidy removal or reduction is needed for effective competition.[1]

However, barring such specific cases, competition and reforms of the government including restrictions on competitive populism

---

[1] How does the subsidy discourage the middle class of India to work against competition-based reforms in the electricity sector is discussed in Santhakumar (2008).

are in the interest of the middle class. But the factors that may cause the emergence of this middle class need to be highlighted.

How Does Such a Middle Class Emerge?

One possibility is to expect the emergence of the middle class as part of economic growth. We have argued in the earlier chapters that there could be economic growth under elite capture, and it may be possible to have some level of economic growth under counter-elite capture or competitive populism. This is possible even if growth-oriented policies are not formulated or enforced adequately under these forms of governance. There could be economic growth even in the absence of such policies in certain contexts. This is so if the capitalist class is in a position to lubricate the system, even if the policies are not growth friendly. Thus, the economic growth which takes place in the domestic economy may create a section of middle class.

An interesting possibility is for the counter-elite capture and competitive populism creating the ground conditions for the emergence of a substantial section of society as the middle class, as economic growth takes place. We have seen the counter-elite capture extending the coverage of private goods transfer to the non-elites. If such transfer helps the poorer sections or non-elites in general to invest in education, then it may enhance their chances of acquiring greater productivity or jobs that offer relatively better incomes, compared to the subsistence wages that they would be getting as mere unskilled labour. This can gradually accelerate their mobility towards the middle class.

Competitive populism accelerates this process of creating a middle class further in two ways. First, a strong competition between elites and counter-elites (or two counter-elites) through electoral democracy will maximise the coverage of private transfer or provision of private goods by incorporating those constituencies excluded under elite and counter-elite regimes. Secondly, competitive populism increases the quantum of such transfer.

As a part of populism, a number of commodities and services (and greater amount of cash transfer) would be distributed to the electorate. Thus, if the limited transfer under a counter-elite rule has not focussed much on education and healthcare, competitive populism is likely to address these limitations. Thus, the chances of enhancing productivity through educational achievements to get a relatively better income for the non-elites are much higher under competitive populism.

It is true that the educational achievements of the poorer sections would be transformed into higher incomes for them only when the economy attracts enough investments and undergoes growth. However, in an open economy setting, a slow pace of growth of the domestic economy may not be such a restraining factor for many people due to the possibilities of migration. Such possibilities have multiplied through the process of globalisation. Barring a few regimes, such as Cuba or North Korea, almost all other countries including some of the failed states have not been able to control the movement of people out of the country, even if they have the most restrictive trade regimes. Hence, many people from the poorer countries migrate and work elsewhere. Such migrant employment opportunities and gradual productivity enhancement, and possibilities of increased income create a middle class even in countries or regions which have failed to attract more investments and undergo substantial economic growth. Thus, globalisation has, by and large, avoided the situation wherein the lack of economic growth in one country prevents the emergence of a middle class there.

There are also countries, such as India, which have opened up their economies during the last three to four decades. This has enhanced the growth of, and income-earning opportunities within, the domestic economy itself. This too has resulted in the creation of a significant section of the middle class in these countries, even though their proportion and distribution (and the electoral influence) may vary in different contexts.

It is the changing attitude of the middle class that may determine the demand for getting out of competitive populism. However, the constellation of parties and other prevailing democratic institutions may determine whether the politicians respond favourably to the demand of the middle class to move away from competitive populism. In order to move out of populism, political competition should be such that the middle class (with the type of demands described in the previous section) is in a position to influence electoral outcome. This is possible even if they are not numerically the majority. This is best possible if the political competition is bi-polar (with two main parties or coalitions), and the competing parties and coalitions are divided, by and large, along the class or income position of the voters. Moreover, the competition should be real with each of the competing parties or coalitions having a reasonable probability of winning the election. There should be at least some sections of middle-class voters who are not willing to follow any one party 'blindly' for ideological or other loyalties. If one party represents the rich and upper middle class, and the other is representing the poor and the lower middle class, the kind of middle class that we describe here may become the median voter. Even otherwise, if the two parties represent some cross-section of voters on the basis of identity or non-economic issues (such as attitude towards nationalism) and/or are driven by the charisma of different leaders; and if their competition is even, then a middle class willing to shift loyalty between two elections can become the deciding factor.

Middle Class and Corruption

The middle class has an interest in opposing corruption. They may incur losses due to monopoly which could be sustained through the cosy relationship between the capitalists and politicians. Since this relationship is the main source of big-ticket corruption, the middle class has an interest in opposing it.

The middle class has a higher demand for public goods due to their relatively higher incomes. Provision of public goods depends not only on capital investments, but also on the observance of certain public rules. Construction of a road is not adequate for safe mobility, but it requires the following or enforcement of traffic rules too. Hence, the middle class has an interest in the enforcement of public rules in general. Although, individually, each may gain from paying a bribe to the enforcement official to avoid observing certain public rules, it may become costly to him/her when everybody else does the same. Hence, they may not like corruption leading to the violation of public rules regarding public goods, externality, etc.

This is true even with regard to those rules made to address asymmetric information related problems in different markets (such as those ensuring the stated quality of the products). Their dependence on such markets is very high so that corruption-led poor enforcement of such rules could be very harmful to them. It is the suppliers (including traders and intermediaries) of such services and products who are likely to benefit from such poor enforcement of information-related rules. Even though there may be some among the middle class who are part of these suppliers (especially service providers and self-employed professionals), the net loss to a middle class household due to poor enforcement of such rules could be substantial due to its participation in different markets for a large number of products and services as customers. Here, too, the 'interest' of the middle class is to avoid corruption in general (even if individually they may indulge in corruption as a supplier of a product or service in a specific market).

Potential entrepreneurs are part of the middle class, even though the currently successful entrepreneurs may not be part of this class. Thus, they are the potential entrants in the supply of commodities and services. Hence, all sorts of entry barriers to these markets are harmful to them. Usually such entry barriers (other than those due to technology or innovation, or due to other factors that create natural monopoly) are likely to be created and sustained through the crony relationship between the political class and the existing suppliers, lubricated through corruption. Hence, the middle class is likely to oppose this form of corruption too.

The middle class may also develop an interest in controlling corruption involving political and governmental functionaries. We have argued that the middle class is less likely to sustain a patronage relationship with the politicians. They may not be comfortable with a feudal provider role of the politician. They are less likely to be active in day-to-day politics, and this may limit the development of a close relationship between them and specific politicians. Some of them may become comfortable with 'politicians as agents' to mediate the delivery of a specific service from the government, such as the provision of a licence to construct a building. However, all among the middle class are less likely to have such a networked relationship with politicians to enable them to get access to such public services. On the other hand, capitalists may develop a more organised relationship with politicians to meet their different needs. The poor too may develop a close relationship with one or the other political representative. Due to these reasons, the middle class may see benefit in gaining access to public services without being intermediated by specific politicians. They may wish to get such services quickly and without discrimination, even without the help of a political intermediary. In the case of specific services, they may pay a bribe to the politician or government official to get the service. However, if the need for bribing causes the delaying of delivery of all such services from the government, it could be costly to them. Thus, they may like to have non-corrupt and quickly delivering public service machinery, even while showing readiness to pay bribe to get a specific public service.

The key difference between the capitalists and middle-class with regard to corruption is the following. The gains for a capitalist (or political class participating in corruption) from a single or a fewer corrupt deals could be so high to compensate for the total of all small losses that he may encounter due to prevalence of corruption in all other spheres of economy. Thus, he may be in a position to 'buy' the functionaries to smoothen his life on other aspects. However, even if a middle class household gains from a specific corrupt deal, the gain from it is less likely to be huge to compensate for all the losses due to corruption in all other walks of life.

However, all sections of middle class may not have the incentive to demand better governance. The source of income may matter. A person can acquire more income and become economically part of middle class through many ways. It can be rents, bribes, higher salaries offered by government jobs in a context where government jobs and the salaries are determined and distributed politically (and not with any economic or market rationale) and so on.

People who acquire higher levels of incomes through such means do not have an incentive to support liberal democracy wherein the government is not allowed to meddle with the economy without any valid economic rationale. Thus, they may continue to support different forms of non-liberal governments which continue to shower them with private gains, which they cannot expect from a competitive economy.

To some extent, this was evident from the limited middle class that evolved in India during the first few decades of its independence. Most of this section comprised of the employees of the government and public sector organisations. Their salaries were fixed by the state without considering the market wage rates. Political involvement in employment creation, appointments, transfers and discipline (or lack of discipline) of employees was very common those days. This section was the only beneficiary of government-supported social security (including life-long pensions), whereas the majority of the people in the country had to find private means for ensuring subsistence during their non-working age. There were publicly provided higher educational institutions catering to their demand, and hence a larger part of the state funds for education was channelised for higher education, neglecting the needs of primary education for the people at large. This section also benefitted from government subsidies provided to water supply, electricity, petroleum fuels and so on, whereas the poor did not benefit from them because they did not have access to such public services. Hence, this middle class was not interested in bringing in ideas of liberal democracy to Indian governance until the seventies and eighties. However, the situation has changed slightly during the last two decades when substantial sections of the middle class have been those who depend on private sector employment.

There could be another section of people whose position went up in the income hierarchy at par with the middle class due to rental incomes. These may include people who hold properties in areas (including cities) which have witnessed economic growth. The land market in India is not adequately competitive, and sections of the society benefit (suffer) from the imperfections and developments driven by non-transparent state policies (such as restriction of land use, and then approvals granted on an ad-hoc basis). There is income growth for other people as well who continue to hold positions which can provide different forms of rent. It may be unrealistic to expect that such people would demand features of liberal democracy, even if they are part of the middle class income-wise.

The exposure to certain social ideas and/or systems too makes a difference. In fact, this exposure is to some extent unavoidable in this era of information technology and globalisation. The individual and human rights available in a developed liberal society becomes attractive to people in other countries only when they are exposed to them. Media discussions, international travel for employment, interaction with foreigners and so on play an important role here. (Such an exposure has also helped the collapse of the Soviet-style governments in the past.) Although such opportunities to interact are increasing today, there are many people in the developing world who can be part of an income-based middle class, but are not exposed to liberal democracy prevalent elsewhere.

Media Helping to Get Out of Populism

It is interesting to see how media works as part of, and facilitates, the evolution of polity from competitive populism to liberal democracy. Based on the socio-economic transition of the society, if sections of people interested in public goods (and not in the widespread provision of subsidised private goods or transfer for such goods), then media may also reflect such a position. This could be true for an anti-corruption position too. Hence, when different forms of media, for competitive reasons or due to the reflection of the interest of substantial sections in society, reflect the aspirations of liberal democracy, they facilitate the transition towards such a system. Since we have defined 'good governance' as a part of this liberal democracy, the way media works towards such good governance also follows this route.

The dominant aspirations of the society can also be shaped to some extent by the media. As noted earlier, even when people are economically at a position to prefer liberal democracy, it need not happen if they are not exposed to the ideas and experiences from elsewhere. Exposure to ideas and experience provide information on institutional opportunities. In the absence of this information, people may not consider pursuing such opportunities as viable tasks. Thus, they may not devote adequate efforts in that direction. (To some extent, this could be the logic of international information advocacy carried out by the communist and non-communist countries during the Cold War.) Even when domestic media does not provide information on liberal-democratic institutional opportunities, some people in these countries may get exposed to functioning of democracy elsewhere in the globalising era through migration, business visits, global media and so on. However, this section is relatively smaller in size even in a country which is an active participant of globalisation. Hence, the role of domestic media in providing information on liberal democratic opportunities to the wider sections of society cannot be underestimated.

These preparations at the level of public discourses and also in the terrain of ideas are which the media helps to achieve. However, when economic or human development conditions are not appropriate, people may not be sensitive to these ideas even if these are widely circulated. Hence, economic or human development and the 'preparations in the terrain of ideas' may have to go hand-in-hand to facilitate the transition towards liberal democracy. In this respect, media plays a simultaneous role, and not one of the follower or pioneer.

Based on the hypothetical arguments presented here regarding the processes that help getting out of competitive populism, we will consider the Indian situation—in different states and at the national level—in the following section.

Moving Out of Competitive Populism: An Empirical Note

We have already seen that competitive populism enabled the space for public action and human development in Indian states, such as Kerala, Tamil Nadu, etc. The strong competition between two coalitions (one led by the INC and the other by the Communist Party of India—Marxist [CPM]) has led to the coverage of private goods and transfer programmes—including the provision of schooling and primary healthcare—to almost all sections of the society in Kerala.

The expansion of school education and public distribution system covering a wide variety of private goods, and the subsidised and widespread provision of other services, such as healthcare, created a relatively healthier and literate population. Although the sluggish investments in domestic economy did not enable industrialisation within Kerala, many Keralites could take up formal sector jobs in other states of India, and also in other countries, ahead of others from India, which are far behind Kerala in terms of human development. This has led to the growth of the service sector within the state, partly driven by the remittances coming to the state from those workers living abroad. Although the state has not strengthened the agricultural and industrial production systems and produced a number of quality jobs within Kerala, many households in Kerala have encountered income growth. The exodus of people finding jobs in West Asia and other countries has continued despite changes in the state (Rajan & Zacharia, 2007). Although there were ups and downs (along with global business cycles), remittances continue to play an important role in Kerala. All these have led to an income growth for a substantial section of Keralites. Kerala has witnessed an economic growth comparable to, or marginally higher than, that in India as a whole from the late nineties onwards, mainly driven by the service sector.

The advances in school education and income growth, and also the awareness of the importance of educational investments as productive capital, have encouraged many households in Kerala to send their children for higher education elsewhere, if not in Kerala. When the successive governments of Kerala took a negative attitude towards the establishment of private engineering and medical colleges within the state, Keralites were the main clients for such colleges in the neighbouring states of Tamil Nadu and Karnataka. Such propensity to invest in higher education by sending children to private colleges in other states was shown not only by the middle class and the richer sections, but also by the lower middle class, marginal farmers and so on. An important reason noted for the farmers' suicides in Kerala was the diversion of loans taken for agricultural purposes for educating daughters and sons in other states in courses, such as nursing (Nair & Menon, 2010). These educational investments also helped Keralites to corner a proportionately greater share of the service sector jobs available in India after its liberalisation in the nineties, and also elsewhere as a part of the current phase of globalisation. Thus, the (lower) middle class sections of Kerala who were expecting a government job in the fifties and sixties, and who benefitted from the supply of such jobs within the state until the eighties and nineties, see their children taking up reasonably paying private sector jobs elsewhere, if not within Kerala. All these have created a middle class within the state less interested in the public provision of private goods by the government within the state.

There are indications that such a middle class is exercising its interests to determine the electoral outcomes in Kerala. The following argument is purely speculative based on one electoral result, and hence should be considered as very tentative. The elections held for the state assembly in 2011 saw a very populist (or the most populist government in the history of Kerala) government voted out of power albeit with a narrow margin. Regarding social support schemes aimed at the poor and the lower middle class, this government made drastic improvements. The cash support given to the aged who were employed in the informal sector (including agricultural sector), widows, etc. was increased by almost three times by this government. Rice was supplied at a very low rate of ₹2 per kilogram to nearly 60 per cent of the households. A large bundle of other food and consumer items (including vegetables) were supplied through different types of government-controlled shops at rates much lower than the market rates through government subsidy. The government spent substantial amounts (around ₹500 crores per annum) on such items, in addition to those distributed through the public distribution system. There were notable improvements in the infrastructure of public schools and government healthcare centres.

There were also many other political advantages for this government. There were no serious allegations of corruption against the ministers of this regime. In addition, the politicians of the opposition coalition were struggling with a number of police inquiries, including those for sexual harassment and corruption. Such allegations against the opposition politicians were catching public attention, especially, immediately before the elections. The chief minister of this regime was a very popular (and populist) politician having support from the lower middle class, poorer sections and backward communities. He was personally taking interest and following up some of the anti-corruption cases against the opposition politicians. He filed a number of public interest litigations in the High Court and Supreme Court of India (in personal capacity) against them. One such prominent opposition politician got one year imprisonment just before the elections. All these have enhanced the public image of the then chief minister.

Despite all these advantages, the front led by him representing the government was voted out of power. There were some areas where the performance of this government was far from satisfactory. Due to the preponderance of social support schemes (and also due to the nature of economic growth of Kerala which did not contribute that much increase in the tax income for the state government), the government of Kerala faced severe fiscal deficit and its debt burden increased drastically (George, 2011). As the government could not invest much in infrastructure and public goods in general, the roads and other common facilities were in disarray during this regime. This was not merely due to the lack of money for investments; even when money was made available through borrowing, the efficiency and effectiveness of public investments were poor. Projects did not move at the desired pace leading to the wastage of money. Even the ruling politicians were aware of the slow pace and inefficiency of governance and public services as a whole. Somehow, these problems did not affect much the delivery of social support and private goods provision. It is relatively easy to provide more money and private goods to the people. Once they are made aware of their entitlements through the media and their demand is created, there would be pressure on the supply channels. It is in the case of public investments and public service delivery that the ineffectiveness of governance made its huge negative impact. Hence, those people interested in having better quality roads and efficient public service delivery became disenchanted with this government.

This seems to have played an important role in the defeat of this government. It showed that a section of society which was not impressed by schemes, such as rice at ₹2 per kilogram or three-time increase in informal sector pension schemes exercised an electoral choice against the ruling coalition leading to its defeat. (It may be noted that this government came to power with a substantial majority, and there was a shift of significant share of voters away from it during the election when it was voted out of power.) It is more likely that such a section belongs to the middle class which is not that much interested in schemes, such as rice at ₹2.[2] It is the same section which sees getting better quality roads and quicker public service more important than getting some private goods at subsidised prices from the government.

One could see a greater focus in the media on the failings of this government in terms of the provision of public infrastructure during its tenure. This is especially so in two major dailies—which has the highest circulation, and also has greater reach among different sections of the society. To some extent, the expansion of social

[2] There were non-economic factors that were in play during that election. In general, the Christians and Muslims were against the coalition in government, whereas majority of the Hindus were for the voted out coalition. However, this has been the picture for a longer period, and each ruling regime comes to power through some cross-voting. Hence, the interesting aspect is that sections of Muslims and Christians which voted for this coalition in 1996 must have decided to vote against it in 2011. There were no serious religious reasons for their shift. There could be economic reasons for this shift. Substantial sections of the Christians and Muslims are not really depending on the state provision that much. However, even the middle and upper middle class sections of the Hindus have greater dependence on the government due to their dominant position in government jobs and among pensioners. The electoral outcome could be crucially determined by the class interest—poor and the lower middle class interested in private goods provision voting for the government, and the middle class interested in infrastructure and public service and improved governance voting against it. It was also evident from that there were greater opposition to the government (and hence their candidates failed) in urban and affluent areas.

security schemes or the provision of food at highly subsidised rates by the previous Left Democratic Front (LDF) government did not get that much attention from these media channels, and the politicians and ministers of that government were complaining about this lack of interest.[3] This was a reflection of the social change in Kerala where a three-time increase in the pension given to an old farm worker may not be of great news value, whereas the potholes on the roads may get considerable media attention. However, the corruption cases or those related to the sexual harassment attracted wider attention, and these worked mostly against the politicians closer to the United Democratic Front (UDF). The election result in 2011 discussed in the previous paragraph was in tune with the changing priorities of the media too.

It may be noted that a vicious cycle of competitive populism decelerating domestic economic development does not limit the possibility of the emergence of a middle class in Kerala. This was due to the open economy providing employment or other income-earning opportunities for the people benefitting from competitive populism through social and human development.

This does not mean that this middle class in Kerala is willing to forgo all the personalised benefits or subsidies that they are currently getting. In those cases where the transfer to them was substantial, their position was ambivalent. For example, the middle class Keralites do not seem to be willing to forego the subsidy that they get for petrol, diesel or LPG. The amounts that they get in this regard could be substantial, and they may be getting it without much sacrifice in terms of quality or without sparing much effort for accessing these services. Thus, there could be opposition to the removal of such subsidies.

Although there has been an income growth for the middle class in Kerala, we have noted that this has not come mainly through domestic industrial development, but through a service sector fuelled by remittances. If the income growth is mainly through domestic (within Kerala) value addition, there would have been

---

[3] This was observed publicly a number of times by T.M. Thomas Isaac, the economist-turned finance minister of this government.

greater incentives to demand better quality infrastructure or public goods. This is so because the lack of such infrastructure and other facilities would have been much more costlier to their income-earning activities. Hence, the current demand for public goods by the middle class would be lesser than that in the situation where most of their income comes from domestic economic activities. This argument is similar to the one which sees lesser incentive for institutional reforms in those countries which depend on the export of primary commodities or natural resources with very little value addition.[4]

If Kerala shows symptoms of moving out of competitive populism as argued here, this can be reckoned as another Kerala model. The 'Kerala model' known in literature is about the achievement of human development even at lower levels of economic development (CDS, 1975). However, we have argued that it is the competitive populism that has helped the achievement of human development in Kerala, and also in other states like Tamil Nadu. In that sense, it is correct to interpret this 'Kerala model' as an early achievement of human development through competitive populism. The current phase of Kerala politics indicates another 'model'. This implies an early transition to liberal democracy in India, and hence this is a model of political transition. It also shows that the previously discussed Kerala model and the current one are interlinked. An early achievement of human development (facilitated by competitive populism) gradually leads to the development of a middle class which may lose interest in such populism, or it shows that societies come out of competitive populism by going through it!

Situation at the National Level

We have seen that such a situation—where the state shows the symptoms of coming out of competitive populism—is visible in Kerala first. This is not surprising because Kerala is the first state

---

[4] For a recent view on this issue, see Ramsay (2011).

which has come out of elite capture, and also got into competitive populism. The early entry into the stage of competitive populism also ensured that Kerala achieved higher levels of human development ahead of other Indian states.

Although there has been a substantial growth of the middle class in India as a whole after the nineties, their share in the whole population may not be more than 25 per cent.[5] They are spread all over the country. Despite their dominance in public discourses, especially in the English-speaking media, they do not have enough electoral clout in most parts of the country.

The current situation at the all India level is competitive populism. This is reflecting in many ways. The regional parties (even if they are ruling their states as elites or counter-elites) started exercising greater power on the national government as coalition partners, and hence they extract a greater share of national public resources for their constituency. (The case of Tamil Nadu and Dravida parties is mentioned often in this regard.) Secondly, national governments have started spending a greater part of the resources for private goods including schooling and healthcare or for the waiver of loans taken by specific sections. A substantial amount of national resources are currently being spent for schooling (*Sarva Shiksha Abhiyan* or Universal Elementary Education), healthcare (National Rural Health Mission—NRHM), rural employment (National Rural Employment Guarantee Act—NREGA), food security and so on. This is also mainly due to the political pressure from below. Such spending has positive benefits in terms of social and human development. There has been significant improvement in indicators, such as literacy rates, enrolment rates, etc. at the national level (Govinda & Bandyopadhyay, 2008; ASER, 2013). Infant mortality rates (IMR) have also come down in many states which were having higher rates of IMR until a decade ago. This is not to say that all human development issues are addressed adequately in India. But the increased government spending in the social sector by the national government has helped, even though there are still certain

---

[5] One account in 2008 puts the middle and higher income groups at 23.3 per cent of the population (Kannan, 2008).

areas and issues that require further action and investments. Thus, the transition to a really competitive democracy and the populist phase is aiding the distribution or transfer of public resources to a wider section of people, and it has a beneficial impact on social and human development. The nation as a whole would continue in this phase for some more time, and it may further accelerate the pace of social or human development.

This has consequences for the fiscal deficits of the country, which could not be controlled by the successive governments according to their own targets. Moreover, even reasonable decisions of the government can be opposed not only by the opposition but also by the constituent parties, and hence these may be delayed or withdrawn. Thus, the logjam in governance or decision making that we see in India today (2011–2012) is also a reflection of competitive populism.

On the other hand, the state of Delhi has the majority of middle class, and they are in a position to influence the election results there. It may be the reason why 'good governance' as indicated by the better provision of public goods and infrastructure seem to be influencing their electoral choices. Thus, a government which seems to be providing these goods and services is re-elected, despite having a strong opposition which can raise populist slogans. It could also be the reason for the Aam Aadmi Party (AAP)—which is the product of a middle class movement against corruption at the national level—to make inroads in Delhi. It was expected beforehand that this new party would have a significant presence in the political scene of Delhi as part of the state elections held in 2013, and it in fact got the maximum number of seats.

In our popular discussions, we may club many things under good governance and some clarity is needed in this regard. For example, people may attribute the re-election of Sheila Dixit (in Delhi) and that of Nitish Kumar (in Bihar) as the evidence to the electorate value of 'good governance'. This is to be interpreted slightly differently within the framework of this book. The 'good governance' in the Bihar context is the better provision of private goods and services (including schooling and primary healthcare) to as many people as possible. Hence, what is visible in Bihar is an effective competitive populism (after getting out of the counter-elite capture of Lalu Prasad Yadav—representing certain sections of the middle caste). The emergence of Nitish Kumar—representing certain other section of middle castes—provided a space for stronger competitive democracy within Bihar. Although the provision of private goods has widened under the counter-elite capture (say, under Lalu Prasad Yadav), it became wider and more effective under competitive democracy with Lalu and Nitish competing. Hence, people started seeing a more effective provision of private goods under Nitish Kumar.

On the other hand, it is not the extended provision of private goods that is reckoned as good governance in Delhi. It is the better provision of infrastructure and public goods. Or the issue of corruption or law and order could become a major electoral issue in Delhi. This does not mean that the middle class in Delhi is willing to forego all private transfers. Their reluctance was seen earlier in the case of electricity tariffs (when they agitated for subsidies in this regard.) Similarly, there may be opposition to the removal of subsidy in the case of LPG and other petroleum fuels. However, people may not take it lightly if the government keeps roads in unusable conditions, although rice is provided at ₹1 or ₹2 to all. Thus, the 'good governance' that catches votes in Delhi is related to public goods.

Based on the observations here, we can think about the response to corruption in India. It is true that the negative attitude towards corruption is on the rise in India as a whole. This is manifested in the popular support (among sections of urban middle class) that the anti-corruption campaign led by Anna Hazare received recently in India. The fact that the government of India was forced to take action against many senior politicians (including ministers) during 2011–2012, and some of them being imprisoned for significant periods were also a reflection of the growing social opposition to corruption in India. Despite these developments, corruption is yet to become a serious issue to vote out politicians in many parts of India. A very apt example is the election victory of a person, who is loyal to a politician or industrialist and is in jail for corrupt deals in a constituency in North Karnataka, against the candidates of the mainstream political parties like the INC and the Bharatiya Janata

Party (BJP).[6] The loyalists of another politician remanded in jail won a number of parliament seats in Andhra Pradesh, defeating the mainstream parties. The elections held in five states after the anti-corruption campaign led by Anna Hazare did not indicate that majority of the voters take corruption as a serious electoral issue. Many sections of Indian voters are yet to see corruption as an important issue to vote against a candidate. People accused in different cases including criminal and corruption cases continue to win elections, especially in rural constituencies and states or areas which are at lower levels of human development.

However, one state, where corruption could tilt the balance in election outcomes in the country is Kerala. There were instances during the last one to two decades when governments or candidates were voted out mainly due to allegations of corruption. In general, big-ticket corruption (involving huge amounts of money) is very rare within the state. This is very different from the situation in many other Indian states, including the neighbouring ones in south India. A politician who was accused of causing a loss to exchequer to the tune of US$ 2500 was put in jail recently even though there were no clear evidence of making personal gains. Although there are corruption scandals in the state, these are either those cases where political decision making have created losses to the public exchequer without evidence of personal gains, or misuses of power leading to very modest gains compared to many cases debated in other parts of India or at the national level. Even in these cases, media, civil society organisations and opposition parties take them up politically and legally to punish the culprits. Public interest litigations are widely used to counter corruption in Kerala. Even if the politicians accused of corruption are not punished immediately by the courts (due to delays), public attention and pressures cause serious political losses for them. For example, they may have to resign political or governmental positions and not be able to contest elections. There are politicians who use anti-corruption campaign as their main political platform, and have

---

[6] This is about the by-election in Bellary in Karnataka when the incumbent was put in jail for cases of corruption related to illegal mining there.

won elections and ruled the state.[7] Some of the politicians use such campaigns to win intra-party battles too. Most of the successive chief ministers in Kerala are known to be non-corrupt or campaigners against corruption, and usually lead modest lives post-tenure since they do not amass wealth during their political careers. This was also in contrast with the picture in a number of Indian states including the neighbouring ones in south India. Hence, one can see a change in the social and political situations in Kerala, where society has become much more vigilant over a period of time against big-ticket corruption by the politicians.

How do we explain the situation in Kerala based on the observations in the way a society develops internal mechanisms to control corruption? The role of the middle class in Kerala is crucial. It is one state where the middle class constitute the majority of the population (with a very small or insignificant share of capitalists and land lords, and with about 20 per cent of the poor by very liberal standards). They do not like collusion between politicians and capitalists, even if they may be indulging in small-time corruption to get a public service quicker and so on. A significant part of this middle class shift in loyalty from one election to other is that no politician or party can hope to win elections with the loyal support base (vote bank) alone. Corruption stories (even if these are milder by national standards) influence this section of middle class, and that is one of the reasons for their antipathy to the ruling coalition in each election. Hence, each of the two opposing coalitions has not ruled the state continuously. Thus, the story about developing incentives to combat corruption for the society described here fits reasonably well with the situation in Kerala.

What about the role of middle class in developed nations? Did they help to move out of competitive populism, as argued here? The historical role of the middle class in the shaping of western developed nations is well debated (O'Boyle, 1966). Yes, the middle class played an important role in socio-economic change there, including the transition towards democracy. One view was to see

---

[7] V. S. Achuthanandan is one such personality, and he used allegations of 'corruption' against the opposition party and also politicians within his party. There are others like A.K. Antony who positions in politics with an anti-corruption image.

the emergent merchant or trading class in the cities of the Europe in the seventeenth and eighteenth centuries as part of the middle class, and they played a role in facilitating the transition away from feudalism. Although the class basis of the French Revolution and its role in facilitating capitalism was debated and contested (Cobban, 1964), it is acknowledged that the middle class comprising of lawyers, peasant proprietors, owners of property in cities was behind the revolution. Hence, the role played by the middle class could be seen in different historical contexts in the developed world.

In general, the middle class (or its different variants) seemed to have accelerated the movement away from elite capture there. The lower middle class and the working class have also facilitated counter-elite assertions. Such assertions and their capture of governments have facilitated the transfer of greater amount of public resources to a wider section of the society, including the institutionalisation of social security. However, there could be some difference in the role of the middle class here compared to that in the developing economies that we have discussed earlier. The economies of the Western developed world could achieve higher levels of incomes even during the elite capture. The early industrialisation and captive access to resources and markets of the colonies could have facilitated this growth. Hence, the need for populism (or the need to provide a wide variety of private goods to people at large as part of the deepening democracy) was not that pronounced there, as in the developing or poorer economies of today. Hence, the middle class may not have encountered the need to moderate populism as much there as in the current developing world. Of course, the middle class has played a role in balancing the needs of social security or distribution on the one hand, and of economic growth or efficiency on the other hand at different stages of the political transition of the Western developed countries.

The progressivism of the United States (US) in the first two decades of the twentieth century (or until the World War) is one notable phenomenon in this regard (Buenker et al., 1986). Improving governance and eliminating corruption formed an important part of the agenda of this period. The monopoly practices and cronyism in business and economy and other sources of inefficiency received attacks from the public and intellectual circles. It also led to the voting rights for women. The social base of this movement was very clearly the middle class. Media too played an important role in exposing corruption in politics and business. There were efforts to bring citizens out of the control of the political bosses (or patronage relationships). Electoral reforms to introduce referendums and recall of the legislators were attempted then. (It is not implied that all the attempts during the progressive era, for example, prohibition or the attraction of some intellectuals towards eugenics, etc., are in tune with our current understanding of liberal democracy.) This progressive era was preceded by the so-called 'Gilded' age which witnessed a number of characteristics: economic growth on the one hand and existence poverty for substantial sections on the other hand, increasing importance of labour unions, expansion of schooling, close competition between political parties and higher turn outs in elections and so on. Hence, this period is characterised by the deepening of democracy, assertion of rights even by non-elites (for example, the working class), intensification of political competition, expansion of private goods distribution, etc. which are closer to the situation of competitive populism in contexts such as in India today. (However, this is not to underplay the historical and socio-economic differences between the current situation in India and the US in the early part of the twentieth century.)

Ill-Governance in the Developed World Today

Those who read the book may have the following question in their mind: Are not there problems of ill-governance in the so-called liberal democracies of the developed world? This is so because the book presumes that the issues of governance in the developing world are likely to be addressed as part of their evolution to liberal democracies. There are issues of governance in such liberal democracies too, and these became much more evident recently as part of the debates and strategies employed by the state to overcome the global financial crisis. These issues can also be analysed within the framework followed in this book. This is discussed briefly in the following section.

These societies have a sizeable middle class ,who could also be the majority (around 60 to 80 per cent of the society). They are, by and large, depending on markets for commodities, jobs, investments, capital, etc. The direct (cash or kind) support received by them for private goods is relatively low (compared to their consumption) even though there exists a reasonable social security for those who fail to make a living on their own. Most of the middle class pays taxes and receive government resources mainly as public goods. The democracy is reasonably well developed so that the rule of law and the democratic processes are not affected much by the conflicts existing within the society. Or the conflicts are operating within the democratic space and without breaking the general rule of law. There are no significant minorities who are excluded from public goods and services, and hence their violent or non-democratic assertion for power is not that much of a serious issue. However, they too face serious problems.

First and foremost is, which can be called, the wealth effect. Since these countries have enjoyed affluence over a reasonably long period of time, such general affluence has influenced their choices. This is nothing surprising. For example, this affluence has impacted their choices on what is a desired wage rate, what is the kind of support needed for people who are jobless, what is the appropriate age for retirement, what is the social security needed for the aged, etc. These choices had an impact on public policies. First of all, there has been some meddling with the markets. For example, the minimum wage rates need not be in tune with the one determined by the markets. There are substantial allocations of public resources for providing social security, medical care, for supporting the poor and so on. This is not surprising and is acceptable in any society. This is especially so if there were adequate public resources through taxation, if the support provided does not affect negatively the incentives of the people to work, if the meddling with the markets does not reduce the competitiveness and if the economic growth is such that it could provide employment to the majority of people (seeking jobs) and also generate adequate taxes for the government. Wealth (accumulated over a period of time), investments in human capital, historical advantages in competition and innovation, and so on helped these countries to continue in this path for a fairly long time. The growing markets in other parts of the world (accessed voluntarily or sometime by means of coercion) also have provided an opportunity for these countries to continue along their development path.

However, there were sources of unsustainable growth in their path. There were countries which borrowed heavily for financing their public expenditure or have suffered serious fiscal problems especially during the recessions, which would arise as part of the inevitable business cycles. The policies used to help the poorer sections were not always incentive compatible. Sometimes policies provided positive feedbacks that led to chaotic situations. It is argued that the cheaper finance offered to the poor and the lower middle class for housing (without much concern for their repayment ability) as part of the support for the poor has led to an unsustainable situation in the US, which has paved the way for financial crisis (Rajan, 2012). There could have been better policy options to support the poor, such as providing subsidised education. However, it is not always easy politically to pick up the best among the policy options, and there could be failures in this regard.

The meddling with market in terms of minimum wage rates or the legally enforced social security for the workers (as in the case of West European countries which had a tradition of social democracy) could go on as long as their economies were competitive. However, globalisation posed serious challenges to their economies. The opening up of markets, the increased participation of the developing world in the global markets, the incentives that this global production has offered to the investors of the developed world to relocate their production and the consequent dependence on the production from the developing world had obvious impacts on the economies of the developed world. The domestic production of those goods and services, which can be imported from, or outsourced to, elsewhere faced severe competition. This led to either increased unemployment and/or the increased cost for the economy and loss of competitiveness. The possibility of migration too has played an important role here. On the one hand, there was limited migration which allowed to bring in cheaper workers. On the other hand, disallowing migration became very costly considering the opportunity costs.

In essence, the social policies designed in the Western developed societies under the influence of the affluence acquired over a sufficiently long period of time become unsustainable today under the influence of globalisation and international migration. Hence, this is leading to newer distributional conflicts in these countries. There is a sizeable section of the (lower and working) middle class which is unwilling to sacrifice the gains received through generous social policies. There is a section of (upper) middle class and affluent which see the continuation of the social policies either as increasing tax rates or government borrowings or reducing the competitiveness of their production systems. It is this conflict and the difficulty to resolve this amicably is reflecting in the governance challenges faced by the developed world today. This also shows the international linkages in terms of human development or the lack of it. If there are countries which continue to be at very low levels of economic development and can supply very cheap labour, they may pose threats to the 'comfortable' distributional equilibrium of the relatively developed world, as the former start participating in the process of globalisation.

One can also hear complaints about pork-barrel politics in the developed world. This is primarily the efforts by the legislators to get a greater allocation of resources (including public projects) to their territorial constituency. Some of them may succeed in this bargaining depending on their power as well as how vulnerable the government is. This too can also lead to a misallocation of resources in the sense that the actual territorial allocation of resources can become different from the one that maximises aggregate social welfare. However, such pork-barrel politics is not without limits. First of all, the limits to such politics are determined by democratic competition—yielding too much into the demand of one would also mean lesser resources for others (or for doing other activities.) In most cases, such politics in the developed world is aimed at public goods or services, and not about the distribution of private goods (or cash transfer) to specific groups of people. Hence, the inefficiency cost imposed by the pork-barrel politics (for competition to get territorial public goods by the legislators) could be lower than that aimed at using public resources for private goods distribution.

In one sense, there is no assurance that even the best among the political institutions can ensure the allocation of resources in an ideal manner (in terms of maximisation of social welfare). What is possible is to minimise the gap between the politically determined (public resource) allocation and the one that maximises social welfare.

Epilogue

We will summarise here a few key lessons, and what can be done to improve governance in different socio-political contexts.

1. Democratisation and good governance need not have a linear positive relationship. There can be a worsening in terms of certain aspects of governance (for example, the provision of public goods or quickness in decision making) as part of the deepening of democracy. However, this should not encourage us to underestimate the importance of democratisation. This is needed for sustainable improvements in development and governance. Hence, even with temporary setbacks in governance, the agenda should be to promote democratisation if the objective is to have sustainable good governance.

2. The use of public resources by the state to distribute private goods is useful at some stage of the socio-economic transformation of the society. This is needed to enhance the basic minimum consumption of the people at large. Political parties may be compelled to do such distribution of private goods competitively at the early stage of democracy and development. Such distribution is likely to improve social and human development outcomes. However, there can be governance problems associated with such distribution.

3. This situation becomes inefficient when such distribution of private goods is carried out even when many people do not need them. This can happen if there are intermediaries who benefit from such distribution, and removing this distortion takes time even after the explicit recognition of this inefficiency. It is not unusual to see the persistence of such inefficient institutions. This can also be due to the general problems associated with political institutions which need

not necessarily reflect the underlying economic changes immediately. The competitive populism changes only when there is a substantial internal constituency which want such a change, and when the signals coming from them are reckoned in the political market.

4. There is no need to be surprised if certain tools to improve good governance working well in certain political contexts become ineffective in certain other contexts. For example, citizen charters which work well in certain contexts need not be used by people in other places where they depend on a patronage relationship with politicians.

5. This should also encourage those who work towards institutional reforms to think about the appropriate strategies to improve governance. In the context of elite capture, the strategy should be to encourage democratisation even if that would mean an anti-elite capture. Then the attempt should be to encourage competitive democracy, and here one should expect (and, to some extent, encourage) populism. The importance of private goods distribution should be understood, but reformers can think about and design transfer schemes that become automatically self-correcting. This is to avoid the creation of mechanisms which survive despite the disappearance of the need for such transfer or the conditions which prevent the evolution of mechanisms to suit the changing socio-economic realities. For example, it is important for the state to see that there are enough schools accessible to all children, but it can be carried out in such a way that some of the schools can be closed down easily as and when there is no demand for them. In summary, the distribution of private goods is important for achieving higher levels of social and human development. One should not expect good governance, in all sense of the term, to accompany as a part of achieving human development. Moreover, it may be very difficult to have any substantial form of good governance for the society as a whole without achieving human development. Hence, in situations where governance is captured by the elites and counter-elites,

encouraging competitive populism is the way forward despite the not-so-nice outcomes in terms of governance as a part of this populism. Or, more broadly expecting a nice path for social change and getting frustrated while seeing that the change sometimes go through nastier turns are not parts of rational thinking.

6. It is in societies which have enjoyed certain levels of human development (mainly through competitive populism) that good governance can become a viable agenda. This may need the building up of a constituency which demands liberal democracy (since good governance defined here is closely related to the prevalence of such democracy). It is the middle class which has the incentive to demand such democracy.

7. It is the absence of such a substantial middle class in most parts of India that creates the persistence of ill-governance. Although a full treatment of this issue cannot be attempted here, the root of this problem lies in the gross failure of India with regard to the spreading of school education for all in its first three to four decades of independent rule. Even today, nearly 45 per cent of the children between 6 and 16 years of age do not complete schooling in the country. This negates, almost completely, the possibility for nearly half of the Indian population to be a part of the middle class that we are talking about. The failure in terms of schooling has direct implications not only for human development, but also for economic growth. When India and China compete for a share of the global market of commodities with similar sizes of population and when half of the working age population do not complete schooling in India, the implications could be noteworthy. It may be noted that the children who complete just school education are more suitable for taking up jobs in the manufacturing sector (as skilled workers). When the size of this work force in India is just half of its potential, its negative impact on the competitiveness of Indian manufacturing, in an open economy context where India competes with not only China but also with other South East and East Asian countries with better educational outcomes, does not require

elaboration. This, in turn, can strengthen the disincentives for completing schooling due to the limited growth (and, hence, the employment opportunities) in manufacturing and encourage more people to continue with less-productive agriculture. This will decelerate, if not throttle, the emergence of a substantial section of the Indian population as the middle class, and can have a negative impact on the efforts to achieve good governance within the country.

8. We have noted that the efforts to improve governance may not make sustainable impact on the wider society in those cases where human development status is not so desirable. In such societies, the enhancement of human development should be the first task. Although this is to take place more organically through competitive populism, outsiders interested in such development can make investments and induce internal actors to work towards higher levels of human development. Economic growth is important, but that alone is woefully inadequate. Adequate investment in education is the most important task. Education of girls is much more important because it will lead not only to improvement in educational outcomes, but also would encourage a favourable demographic transition, and both these are important for achieving higher levels of human development.

9. Hence, in situations where the middle class is not substantial, the efforts should be aimed at creating them. However, where many people have adequate incomes so as to call them the middle class, but are not yet 'modern' to demand liberal democracy, the effort should be on such modernisation to create this demand. In those cases where the middle class is trapped in populist delivery of private goods by the state, the effort should be to create incentives and institutions that enable them to come out. In those cases where the demands of the middle class are not getting reflected in the political decision making, the efforts should be to make the 'political competition' effective. Hence, achieving good or better governance requires efforts along multiple directions, and

the importance of each one of them may vary depending on the specific context.

10. This book emphasises the importance of politicisation in achieving good governance. Hence, it does not see technical or economic prescriptions to improve governance working well in contexts where appropriate political transition (which is closely related to the distribution of resources and power within the society) has not taken place. However, this does not mean that economics or a rational choice framework is irrelevant in understanding the institutional or political constraints against improving governance. In fact, the analysis in the book shows that such a framework can be used to understand the incentives of individuals and groups which facilitate a certain type of allocation of public resources within the society, and how this may work against achieving good governance. It also shows how these incentives may change over a period of time, and also the conditions under which it may enable a public-resource allocation which facilitates good governance. Although there are political studies (and political criticisms) on the economic approach to good governance, these rarely come out with a systematic explanation of the barriers and a prediction of the dynamics of political transition. On the other hand, this book highlights not only the limitations of an economic prescription of good governance which neglects the political transition, but also the potentially real barriers against improving governance and how these may be overcome.

Bibliography

Acemoglu, A., Johnson, S., & Robinson, J. A. (2001). The colonial origins of comparative development: An empirical investigation. *The American Economic Review, 91*(5), 1369–1401.

Alavi, H. (1972). The state in post-colonial societies: Pakistan and Bangladesh. *New Left Review*, I/74, 59–81.

Annual Status of Education Report (rural). (2013). (Facilitated by Pratham), New Delhi: ASER.

Bagchi, A. K. (1982). *The political economy of underdevelopment.* Cambridge: Cambridge University Press.

Banerjee, A. V., & Newman, A.F. (1993). Occupational choice and the process of development. *Journal of Political Economy, 10*(2), 274–299.

Bardhan, P. (1984). *Political economy of development in India.* Oxford: Oxford University Press.

Bardhan, P., Mitra, S., Mukherjee, D., & Sarkar, A. (28 February, 2009). Local democracy and clientelism: Implications for political stability in West Bengal. *Economic and Political Weekly, 44*, 46–58.

Bhattacharyya, D. (2009). Of controls and factions: Changing 'party society' in rural West Bengal. *Economic and Political Weekly, 44*(9), 59–69.

Buenker, J. D., Burnham, J. C., & Crunden R. M. (1986). *Progressivism.* Cambridge, Massachusetts: Schenkman Publishing Company.

CDS (Centre for Development Studies). (1975). *Poverty, unemployment and development: A case study of selected issues with special reference to Kerala.* New York: Department of Economic and Social Affairs, United Nations.

———. (2009). *E-governance in local governments of Kerala: Analyzing institutional issues.* Trivandrum: CDS.

Chatterjee, P. (2009). The coming crisis in West Bengal. *Economic and Political Weekly, 44*(9), 43–45.

Cobban, A. (1964). *The social interpretation of the French Revolution.* Cambridge: Cambridge University Press.

Crosby, A. (1986). *Ecological imperialism: The biological expansion of Europe 900–1900.* New York: Cambridge University Press.

Dixit, A. (2009). Governance, institutions and economic activity. *American Economic Review, 99*(1), 5–24.

Dornbush R., & Edwards, S. (Eds) (1991). *The macroeconomics of populism in Latin America.* Chicago: The University of Chicago Press.

Easterly, W., & Levine, R. (1997). Africa's growth tragedy: Policies and ethnic divisions. *Quarterly Journal of Economics, 112*(4), 1203–1250.

George, K. K. (2011). *Kerala economy: Growth, structure, strength and weakness.* Working Paper No. 25., Kochi: Centre for Socioeconomic and Environmental Studies.

Govinda, R., & Bandyopadhyay, M. (2008). *Achieving universal elementary education in India: Enhancing access with equity*. New Delhi: National University of Education Planning and Administration.

Hayami, Y., & Godo, Y. (1997/2010). *Development economics*. New Delhi: Oxford University Press.

Hout, W. (Ed.) (2008). *Governance and the depoliticisation of development*. New York: Taylor & Francis.

Isaac, T. M. T., & Ramakumar, R. (2006). Why do the states not spend? *Economic and Political Weekly, 46*(48), 4972.

Jeffrey, R. (2008). *Coalitions and consequences: Learnership and leadership in India: 1948-2008*, ASARC Working Paper (https://crawford.anu.edu.au/acde/asarc/pdf/papers/2008/WP2008_02.pdf).

Kannan, K. P. (2008). *Dualism, informality and social inequality: An informal economy perspective of the challenge of inclusive development in India*, Presidential Address, 50th Annual Conference of the Indian Society of Labour Economics, Lucknow, December 13–15.

Katzenstein, M. F. (1979). *Ethnicity and equality: The Shiv Sena party and preferential policies in Bombay*. Ithaca, NY: Cornell University Press.

Kitschelt, H. & Wilkinson, S.I. (Eds) (2007). *Patrons, clients and policies*. Cambridge: Cambridge University Press.

Kurien, J. (1995). The Kerala model: Its central tendency and the outlier. *Social Scientist, 23*(1–3), 70–90.

La Porta, R., Lopez-de-Silanes, F., Shleifer, A., & Vishny, R. W. (1998). Law and finance. *Journal of Political Economy, 106*, 1113–1155.

Lieten, G. K. (September 28, 1996). Panchayats in western Uttar Pradesh. *Economic and Political Weekly, 31*, 2700–2705.

Lundahl, M. (1983). *Political economy of disaster and underdevelopment*. London: Routledge.

Magraw, R. (1983). *France 1815–1914*. Oxford: Oxford University Press.

Madras Institute of Development Studies. (1988). *Tamil Nadu economy*. Madras: MIDS.

Mukund, K. (1998). *Andhra Pradesh economy in transition*. Hyderabad: Centre for Economic and Social Studies.

Nair, K. N., & Menon, V. (2010). Distress, debt, and suicides among farmer households. In D. N. Reddy & S. Mishra (Eds), *Agrarian crisis* (pp. 230–260). New Delhi: Oxford India.

North, D. C., Summerhill, W., & Weingast, B. (1998). Unpublished Manuscript. *Order, disorder and economic change: Latin America vs North America*. Hoover Institution, Stanford University.

Nossiter, T. N. (1982). *Communism in Kerala: A study in political adaptation*. London: C. Hurst & Co. Publishers.

O'Boyle, L. (1966). The middle class in Western Europe, 1815–1848, *The American Historical Review, 71*(3), 826.

Poulantzas, N. (1969). The problem of the capitalist state. *New Left Review, 58*, 67–78.

Prabhu, S. (2001). Economic reform and social sector development: A study of two Indian states. New Delhi: SAGE.

Raj, K.N., & Tharakan, M. (1983). Agrarian reform in Kerala and its impact on the rural economy: A preliminary assessment. In Ajit Kumar Ghose (Ed.), *Agrarian reform in contemporary developing countries* (pp. 31–42), London and New York: Groom Helm and St. Martin's Press.

Rajan, R. (2012). The true lessons of the financial crisis: The West can't borrow and spend its way to recovery, *Foreign Affairs*, May/June 2012 Issue. Retrieved from http://www.foreignaffairs.com/articles/134863/raghuram-g-rajan/the-true-lessons-of-the-recession.

Rajan, S. I., & Zachariah, K.C. (2007). Remittances and its impact on the Kerala economy and society.

Ramachandran, V. K. (1997). On Kerala's development achievements. In Sen, A. & Dreze, J. (Eds), *Indian development: Selected regional perspectives* (pp. 205–356). Oxford: Oxford University Press.

Ramsay, K. W. (2011). Revisiting the resource curse: Natural disasters, the price of oil, and democracy, *International Organization*, *65*, 507–529.

Ratcliffe, J. (1978). Social justice and the demographic transition: Lessons from India's Kerala state. *International Journal of Health Services*, *8*(1), 123–144.

Santhakumar, V. (2003). The impact of distribution of costs and benefits of non-reform: A case study of power sector reforms in Kerala between 1996 and 2000. *Economic and Political Weekly*, *38*(2), 147–154.

Santhakumar, V. (2008). *Analyzing social opposition to reforms: Evidence from Indian electricity sector*. New Delhi: SAGE.

Sen, A., & Dreze, J. (Eds) (1989). *Hunger and public action*. Oxford: Clarendon Press.

Service, E. R. (1978). Classical and modern theories on the origins of government. In Cohen, R. & Service, E. R. (Eds), *Origins of the state: The anthropology of political evolution* (pp. 21–34). Philadelphia, PA: ISHI.

Suri, K. C. (2003). Andhra Pradesh: From populism to pragmatism. *Journal of Indian School of Political Economy*, *15*(1&2), 45–77.

Wynia, G. (1984). *The politics of Latin American development* (2nd ed.). Cambridge: Cambridge University Press.

Index

About the Author

V. Santhakumar is currently Professor, Azim Premji University, Bangalore. He had been a faculty, for 15 years (1996–2011), and is currently a Visiting Professor at the Centre for Development Studies, Trivandrum. He worked as a full-time volunteer in a major non-governmental organisation called Kerala Sasthra Sahithya Parishad. He completed doctoral research from the Indian Institute of Technology, Madras. He has held postdoctoral scholarships at the Wageningen Agricultural University, Netherlands, and Vanderbilt University, United States.

V. Santhakumar has also carried out a number of consultant assignments for the Asian Development Bank, United Nations Environment Programme and United Nations Development Programme in different states of India, and in Tajikistan, Palestine, Laos and so on. He has received the research medal and the outstanding research award of the Global Development Network, during its initial years. He specialises in institutional issues of environment, natural resources, energy and infrastructure. In addition to publishing in international journals, he has authored *Analysing Social Opposition to Reforms* (2008), *Economic Analysis of Institutions: A Practical Guide* (2011) and *Economics in Action: An Easy Guide for Development Practitioners* (2013)—all published by SAGE India. He has also co-edited the two-volume series on *Law and Economics* (2013) published by SAGE India.